Medicine Stories

*History, Culture and
the Politics of Integrity*

Aurora Levins Morales

South End Press
Cambridge, MA

Cover illustration by Ricardo Levins Morales
Text design and production by the South End Press collective
Printed in the U.S.A. on acid-free paper
First edition

Library of Congress Cataloging-in-Publication Data

South End Press, 7 Brookline Street, #1, Cambridge, MA 02139
04 03 02 01 00 99 98   1 2 3 4 5 6 7

For my father, Richard Levins,
who taught me there are no bad people, only bad choices,
and to joyfully embrace complexity,
and whose faith in people and their creativity is as deep and wide as
history

Contents

Acknowledgements

Political and creative thinking always takes place in community. This book is the product of thousands of conversations taking place over decades—with individuals over tea and on the way to events, in meetings hashing out strategy and dividing tasks, in dialogue with audiences at readings and lectures and in internal conversation with people whose voices I heard on the radio or whose writing I stumbled on. There are, however, some people whose ongoing conversations with me over the years have enriched and challenged my thinking so consistently that I always consult them at least in my mind. My father's vision, creativity, chutzpah and obvious enjoyment of political engagement is the environment in which I became an activist and a thinker. My mother's finely honed honesty and insistence on authenticity, accuracy and accountability and her ability to name the problem clearly have kept me sharp. Being writers together has strengthened and empowered my voice.

Thanks to my brother Ricardo, co-conspirator extraordinaire in the world of radical art and history-telling and to my brother Alejandro for his unwavering belief in me and my projects. To Staci Haines for brilliance and courage in the work of crafting a repoliticized movement of sexual abuse survivors and for five-hour talks over Pad Thai and to all the other brave participants of that effort. To all the progressive Jewish communities and networks I've had the honor of being part of for publicly insisting that our Jewishness be radical and our radicalism Jewish. To the tribe of womanist-of-color writers and thinkers whose emergence into public and published view during my coming of age has so profoundly shaped my belief in my right to be here and to speak aloud.

To my camaradas in the Puerto Rican Studies Association, my hermanas of the Latina Feminist Comparative Research Group, all the past and present members of the Jews Shmooze. Thanks to my students for the opportunities to learn, practice and refine my thinking.

To my many teachers and companions in Re-evaluation Counseling, especially to Ricky Shervover Marcuse, Alison Ehara-Brown, Cherie Brown, Patti Wipfler, David Jernigan, Diane Balser, Lorenzo García, Jenny Helbraun, Victor Lewis, Paula Buel, Julie Saxe, Michael Taller and Susan Stebbins for bold, practical and whole-human visions of liberation.

To Becky Logan, co-historian and cemetary crawler, for loving archives and detective work as much as I do and always being eager to talk shop. To Rebecca Conard, Minnie Bruce Pratt, Leslie Feinberg, Peter Rachleff, Dave Roediger, Shari Geistfeld, Aya de León, Ruth Mahany, Nina Jo Smith, Gabriel Melendez and many others for specific encouragement to do my work.

My deep appreciation to Lori Kandels whose infinite respect, intelligence, skill and tenderness as a therapist carried me through both healing and theorizing my experiences of torture.

To SpeakOut! Speakers and Artists and South End Press for initiating this project and to Loie Hayes for being a sensitive and flexible editor. To Elizabeth Garcia, my assistant, whose orderly mind and promotional assertiveness have kept my head above water through times of insolvency and exhaustion.

Thanks to my family for their loving support of me. To my daughter Alicia for bright questions, common sense, indignation about injustice, her pride in her mother and lots of cuddling. To my husband and compañero Barry Kleider for helping me bring the vision home and for the courage, passion, joy and loving persistence he brings to reinventing marriage. To Jeremy Beckel-Kleider for informing me that I'm a step-step-mother and doing the long distance two-step with me.

Finally, I thank Spirit for blessing me with this task and for the privilege of living in interesting times, and all the spirits who came before me for giving me something to go on.

~Introduction

The Political is Personal

How I Wrote This Book

The essays in this book are about the core issues in my life. They come out of a twenty-year practice of activism through which I have tried to integrate healing myself and healing the world. In particular, they come out of the last seven years, a time of intense personal and political growth. During this period I decided to strengthen my skills as an artist by becoming a historian. I spent six years in graduate school, researching and writing about the histories of Puerto Rican women and many other, interrelated histories. During that same period I did intensive personal healing work to recover from several years of severe sexual, physical and psychological abuse during my childhood.

I started graduate school and therapy within two weeks of each other because at some level I understood that the two processes were intimately linked. Politicizing the abuse, coming to understand its social context and meaning is a large part of what made it possible to recover; and personalizing history, making the vast sweep of people and events intimate and real, is part of what makes it potent, usable, medicinal. But more than that, I understood that excavating and revealing the truth about my experiences of abuse, and the sense of empowerment and release that process brought me, was the same process as excavating and telling the truth about the centuries of invasion, enslavement, patriarchal rule, accommodation, collaboration and resistance. The healing came from the same source.

For me, the process of story, of bearing witness, has been crucial for both. Whether it takes place in the supposedly private context of sexual abuse or the public and allegedly impersonal arenas of colonialism, patriarchy or a profoundly racist class society, the traumatic experience of being dehumanized and exploited strips people of their stories, of the explanations that make sense of their lives. Instead, it imposes on us the self-justifying mythologies of the perpetrators. We are left adrift, the connection between cause and effect severed so that we are unable to identify the sources of our pain.

Individual abuse and collective oppression are not different things, or even different orders of magnitude. They are different views of the same creature, varying only in how we accommodate to them. Child sexual abuse is explained as a psychological twist in the perpetrator; gang violence and hate crimes as psycho-sociological compounds of collective frustration, group dynamics and personal insecurities and aggressiveness; the massive perpetrations of poverty, pillage and war as byproducts of the efficient organization of society. But abuse is the local eruption of systemic oppression, and oppression the accumulation of millions of small systematic abuses.

However the abuse is perpetrated, the result is the same: abuse does not make sense in the context of our humanity, so when we are abused, we must either find an explanation that restores our dignity or we will at some level accept that we are less than human and lose ourselves, and our capacity to resist, in the experience of victimhood.

I call the work I do "cultural activism" because it does battle in the arena of culture, over the stories we tell ourselves and each other of why the world is as it is. It's a struggle for the imaginations of oppressed people, for our capacity to see ourselves as human when we are being treated inhumanely. Cultural activism is not separate from the work of organizing people to do specific things. In fact, successful organizing depends on this transformation of vision; the most significant outcome of most organizing campaigns is the transformation that takes place in people who participate.

It is short-sighted and self-defeating to see cultural work of this kind as "soft" politics. The reality is that when we are unable to mobilize people on their own behalf, the difficulty is usually at the level of vision. Either we ourselves have been unable to see the people with whom we are working as fully human and have treated them as victims instead of allies, or we have failed to engage their imaginations and spirits powerfully enough. Cultural work, the work of infusing people's imaginations with possibility, with the belief in a bigger future, is the essential fuel of revolutionary fire. That is what this book is about—the capturing of imagination, the restoration of wholeness and a sense of dignity; the nitty-gritty of how to bring complexity into places where we are offered simplistic and shallow explanations, and how to strip artificial complication from the straightforward; how to name and reclaim, over and over, the connections we are taught to ignore, the dynamics we are told do not exist.

What I am arguing for in these essays is a politics of integrity, of being whole. A political practice that sacrifices neither the global nor the local, ignores neither the institutional power structures nor their most personal impact on the lives of individual people. That integrates what oppression keeps fracturing. That restores connections, not only in that future we dream of, but right here in the gory, tumultuous, hopeful, messy and inconsistent present.

*****

The essays in this book vary in length, from long pieces developed over a significant period of time to very short think pieces originally written as parts of class or workshop lectures. The first section of *Medicine Stories* is about history itself, about the struggle over who has the authority to tell the stories that define us. It's about imperial history, the history made by people with agendas of domination and used to strip those targeted for domination of hope; and about radical history, what I call medicinal history, which does the opposite, distilling a legacy of pride, hope and rebellion from ordinary people's lives.

"False Memories: Trauma and Liberation" is about the traumatic nature of oppression, the need to bring together what we know from the most individual and the most collective places of violence. It is about how the processes of recovery we have come to understand through the politicized feminist psychology of the anti-rape, anti-battering and incest survivor movements, as well as from war veterans and survivors of political torture, are the same processes needed for collective recovery. I examine some of the fierce contemporary battles for control of individual and collective memory and the ways in which those battles lie at the heart of both personal and community struggles to take ourselves back from ongoing traumatic abuses. Finally, it is about how the work of historians and artists to research, reinterpret and popularize new visions of history contributes to collective healing in ways that are deeply radicalizing. In "The Historian as Curandera" I discuss in detail my own project to retell Puerto Rican history through the lives of women and the specific ways I approached this task in order to make effective medicine for the cultural and psychological effects of poverty, enslavement, intense racism and patriarchal colonial rule.

In "The Tribe of Guarayamín" I write about some of the pitfalls of doing history with an agenda without cleaning house first. In particular, how the hunger for validation can pull us to duplicate in our own versions of history the ideas of purity and domination that fill imperial histories, using the master's tools not to dismantle the master's house, but to redecorate it.

"Nightflying: Transforming Traumatic Memory" asks questions about the unbearable in history, how it impacts our view of the world and what we may be able to learn from being willing to examine the horrific. What do we miss from avoiding the most overtly violent moments of our past? Our collective memory and silence about such events exerts social control long after the events are officially over. In "Nightflying" I look specifically at the European witch persecutions as an example of traumatic history. What impact does the history of such overtly woman-hating persecution have on contemporary women? Why is it rarely taught about in any serious or comprehensive way, even in Women's Studies courses? What are we protecting ourselves from examining? "The Politics of Childhood" looks at another kind of denial, in which the oppression of an immense constituency—furthermore, one through which we all pass—is trivialized and rendered invisible. I talk about the ways in which the social conditions of childhood keep the wheels of inequality turning and why I believe the current upsurge in children's liberation movements is critical to the creation of a just world.

The second section, "Speaking in Tongues," is about language, and particularly how privileged language is used to silence and ridicule the authentic stories of everyone else. The three essays address specific ways in which I have had to struggle for the right to speak in my own voice against invalidations based in language.

"On Not Writing English" deals with class elitism and my experiences, as a woman of color, with white feminist academic editors who have attempted to "purify" my writing by making it less personal and direct and by replacing its orally based rhythms with the more formal, Latinate language they find comfortable.

"Forked Tongues: On Not Writing Spanish" was originally a talk I gave at a conference of Puerto Rican writers held in Puerto Rico during "Semana de la lengua" or "Week of the Language" shortly after a "Spanish only" resolution was passed on the island. In it I reject ideas of nationalist cultural purity, celebrate the vibrant impurity of Puerto Rican Spanish, of which English is only another layer, and talk about how the work of U.S. Puerto Rican writers opens up new possibilities for the island as well as the immigrant communities.

The last essay in this section is called "Certified Organic Intellectual: On Not Being Postmodern." I have a lot more to say about the politics of postmodernism than there is room for here. In this essay I've chosen to write mostly about my own non-academic intellectual traditions and how they shape my use of language; and to look at how the pervasive, practically mandatory, use of postmodernist jargon in higher education damages the sense of intellectual validity of students and faculty alike, especially women, people of color and working-class people.

I should also say that I have deliberately chosen to write this book in straightforward prose because I refuse to participate in making people feel stupid, and to demonstrate that complex and sophisticated ideas do not require specialized language for their expression; in fact, such language is often effectively used to disguise thinness of content, a lack of intellectual complexity and/or originality.

Part three, "Raíces," or roots, is, in a sense, about the realities and myths of identity politics, a term that lumps together the most militantly ethnocentric nationalism with the whole range of attempts to politicize the discussion of ethnicity. "Raícism: Rootedness as Spiritual and Political Practice" proposes some ways to honestly investigate and understand our historical relationships to our own cultural/ethnic identities and embrace with integrity the full complexity of who we are. "What Race Isn't: Teaching Racism" is about teaching about racism, and the need to hold the tension between the devastating reality of racism and the unreality of race. In "Puerto Ricans and Jews" I try to do just that, as I examine the intricate ways in which ethnicity and class, opportunism and solidarity, immigration and assimilation have shaped relations between my two peoples, with some agendas for further investigation. Section four, "Privilege and Loss," contains three essays about very different aspects of privilege and the costs of accepting it. "Class, Privilege and Loss" is about the fraudulent promises of class privilege. Based on work I've been doing with a support group for progressive middle-class people, I talk about what we give up in exchange for the illusions of privilege, some of the historic choices to surrender relationships of solidarity for apparent security, and how to remake those decisions, both as individuals and collectively.

"Nadie la tiene: Land, Ecology and Nationalism" was written for a special issue of the Jewish feminist journal *Bridges* focusing on Jewish women's relationships to land. Starting with the histories of my own family, I talk about the land my hacendado ancestors built class privilege on, the land my Jewish ancestors farmed and fled, and our own thirty-four acres of Puerto Rican mountaintop. I also explore the contradictions between land as an exploited political symbol in nationalist rhetoric, land as economic resource and land as living presence, and the tensions between ecology and ownership, profitability and cultural rootedness.

"Torturers" grows from my own experience as a torture survivor and from my deepest beliefs about the human capacity to heal. It is a call for a politics of inclusion that abandons no-one, and begins with those it is hardest for us to think about with compassion—the professional perpetrators of atrocities. I call on us all for bolder, more visionary approaches to the constituency of the most spiritually damaged. If we are not to perpetuate the cycles of violence, if we are not to become the people we oppose, we need to understand how such people are created and intervene on their behalf.

The final section, "Integrity," is about wholeness, about living a politics of integrity in our real lives. "Radical Pleasures: Sex and the End of Victimhood" is about the power to be found in reclaiming and healing wounded sexuality, not solely as a personal act of recovery for the abused, but also as a collective political act that can transform the ways in which we talk about sexual abuse. It is also about giving up the culture of victimhood in every arena of our lives. "Circle Unbroken: The Politics of Inclusion" is about making and acting upon an uncompromising commitment against all forms of injustice. I talk about the ways that organizing on the basis of everything, and on behalf of everyone, is actually much easier than single-issue activism. It both requires and provides a higher level of integrity and hopefulness.

"Walking the Talk, Dancing to the Music: The Sustainable Activist Life" is about how to live a sustainable activist life over the course of many decades. Ending where I began, with the integration of collective and individual liberation, I talk about the elements of cultural, spiritual and personal life that give people the staying power to grapple with injustice, cruelty and greed without becoming cynical. Lifelong activists need to cultivate our faith in people and find ways to balance clarity and hope, persistence and trust, anger and joyous pleasure, and learn to live simultaneously in the vision of what is possible and the reality of what is.

~Historian as Curandera

False Memories

Trauma and Liberation

---

*"What would happen if one woman told the truth about her life?
The world would split open."*

Muriel Rukeyser

~*1*~

The structures of unequal power are many-layered and complex in the ways they function in the world. But at its root, oppression is really quite simple. It's about looting. The rest is made up of the rules and institutions, rituals and agreements, mythologies, rationales and overt bullying by means of which small groups of people keep a firm grasp on way more than their share of the world's resources.

But just as intense heat makes ripples and waves that distort our view of the road and give us the illusion of water when there is only hot asphalt, oppression of any kind tugs at the culture around it, distorting our view of the naked exercise of power, normalizing it so that it appears natural and tolerable. Making it look like the reason we're thirsty is not that we're being denied water, but our own lack of initiative in the midst of plenty.

Those with privilege cover up the bare bones of what they're up to with all kinds of elaborate theories and justifications, until they persuade themselves that living at the expense of other people is the right thing to do, a luxury they have earned by excellence, the natural way of life, the righteous and inevitable order of things. Some go so far as to convince themselves that exploitation is not only justifiable but a kind and compassionate expression of their superiority. These lies saturate our culture in ways both subtle and obvious.

The slavers who kidnapped millions of West African people, transported them under conditions that made a third of them die of the journey, gang-raped and tortured them, then sold them into lifelong unpaid labor—and the slave owners who bought them, worked them mercilessly, again raped them at will, routinely tortured them as punishment, sometimes for acts of resistance as small as looking a white man in the eye, sometimes merely to emphasize their power, and who, because of the work of slaves, led lives of leisure—found endless ways to justify their behavior, even to the extent of claiming that slavery was a civilizing influence on the lives of the enslaved. In a massive act of projection, they often described the African people who did every stitch of their work for them as lazy; seriously believed that slaves needed European people to set them tasks and make them useful. They even fantasized that had Europeans not enslaved them, African peoples would have died off from their inability to fend for themselves. After abolition, many ex-slave holders complained of the ingratitude of their former captives.

Or consider the almost hallucinatory fantasies of wealthy members of Congress that teenage African-American welfare mothers, a small minority of the welfare-receiving population, and consuming a minuscule fraction of the public budget, are responsible for bankrupting the economy, growing rich at public expense by having babies in order to pad their AFDC checks. Excluded from decent employment and denied the most basic necessities so as not to slow down the astronomical rise in income of the top 10 percent, these young women are held publicly accountable for the pillaging of our common resources by the greedy.

The mechanism is the same whether we talk about individual or collective atrocities. Feminist psychologist Judith Herman describes the ways in which perpetrators seek to control disclosures of abuse:

> In order to escape accountability for his crimes, the perpetrator does everything in his power to promote forgetting. Secrecy and silence are the perpetrator's first line of defense. If secrecy fails, the perpetrator attacks the credibility of his victim. If he cannot silence her absolutely, he tries to make sure no-one listens. To this end, he marshals an impressive array of arguments, from the most blatant denial to the most sophisticated and elegant rationalization. After every atrocity one can expect to hear the same predictable apologies: it never happened; the victim lies; the victim exaggerates; the victim brought it on herself; and in any case it is time to forget the past and move on. The more powerful the perpetrator, the greater his prerogative to name and define reality, and the more completely his arguments prevail.[1]

Similarly, collective abuses—from the violence of poverty to police brutality, from colonial invasion to slavery to genocide—are denied, dismissed, blamed on the victims and erased from public discussion.

Such lies are part of the apparatus that justifies the massive accumulation by a few people of wealth beyond any human individual's needs. In order for the thing to work, the humanity of almost everyone must somehow be made invisible. Who could bear to hold privilege that meant the suffering and death of others if they had not been trained from early childhood to see these others as not real? Who would tolerate, for even an hour, the inhuman conditions imposed by the privileged, if they had not been trained from early childhood to feel themselves not fully entitled to life?[2]

The culture that inequality creates around itself is saturated with pain, confusion, alienation, a sense of the unreality of our own experience and that of others, an inability to name the abuses we experience, perpetrate and witness on a daily basis. Part of what leaves us numb is the massive scale on which these abuses occur. We are a society of people living in a state of post-traumatic shock: amnesiac, dissociated, continually distracting ourselves from the repetitive injuries of widespread collective violence.

When individual people are abused, the events themselves become a story of our worthlessness, of our deserving no better. We must struggle to re-create the shattered knowledge of our humanity. It is in retelling the stories of victimization, recasting our roles from subhuman scapegoats to beings full of dignity and courage, that this becomes possible. The struggle we engage in is over whose story will triumph, the rapist's story or the raped woman's, the child abuser's or the child's, the stories of bigoted police officers or those of families of color whose children are being murdered. The stories of perpetrators are full of lies and justifications, full of that same projection that holds the abused responsible for her abuse. The stories of the abused are full of dangerous, subversive revelations that undermine the whole fabric of inequality.

~2~

Memory, individual and collective, is clearly a significant site of social struggle. The "false memory" movement that seeks to deny authority over memory to sexual abuse survivors; escalating attacks on multicultural education, particularly in the teaching of history; revisions of Holocaust history that deny it took place, are all examples of current public debates over control of memory. All involve a backlash against powerful popular movements to reclaim authority.

The past is a powerful resource with which to explain and justify the present and create agendas for the future. The frequency with which adult women report that they were sexually abused by their families as children requires a story. That story must either radically redefine how the nature of family is understood in popular culture, or locate responsibility for these reports in the psyches of the women making them. Feminists have sought to do the first, and the false memory movement has sought, by inventing a new category of invalid experience, to do the latter.

Multicultural education—particularly the revision of history and literature curricula to include the presence and voices of women, people of color, poor and working-class people, lesbian, gay, bisexual and transgendered people—grew out of broad social movements that erupted in this country during the 1960s, '70s and early '80s and that responded to decolonization processes internationally. Women's Studies, Ethnic Studies, LGBT Studies and the various ways in which working-class culture and thought have been slipped into curricula have presented major challenges to elite control of knowledge, to what story is told about U.S. society.

As the movements that created such academic disciplines have weakened, attacks on multiculturalism have increased. As in the case of the false memory movement, the privileged accuse the disempowered of oppressing them. Multiculturalism violates the "freedom" of privileged white heterosexual men by forcing them to participate in a world in which their interests and perceptions are not the exclusive priority of everyone.

Those who have considered it their private preserve to decide what is and isn't knowledge, art or culture have persuaded themselves that our determination to define these things for ourselves is a threat to their interests. In reality, it's their best chance for survival. The narrow mythologies upon which they have based their lives will not see them through another century. The denial of our interrelatedness is killing this planet and too many of its people.

Holocaust revision, the story that accuses Jews of manufacturing the history of Nazi atrocities and genocide as a bid for power and "special privileges," uses a similar reversal whereby Nazi Germany becomes the victim of those Jews who survived the attempt to exterminate them. The Holocaust is searing evidence of what theories of genetic inferiority, what the dehumanizing of whole populations can bring about. As we experience a rising visibility and popularity of such ideologies once again, both at the level of neo-Nazi organizing and within scientific debates on the role of genetics in shaping our lives, there is a clear incentive for supporters of these ideologies to erase the well-documented and horrifying realities of the Holocaust and replace them with an account that again places the story in the psyche of the victim, rather than in the world.

For Jews, for incest survivors, for all the people systematically excluded from official histories, the issue is the same. Oppression, whether on the massive social scale of the Holocaust or in the power abuses of incest within one home, is deeply traumatic. Traumatized individuals and communities experience themselves as dehumanized by abuse. The story told by the actions of the perpetrators is that those who are targeted are not human beings. Evidence that such a belief is a central ingredient in oppressor ideology, and essential, in fact, to carrying out their programs, is to be found everywhere, from Nazi propaganda to slave-holder mythology to the persistent belief that women ask for and enjoy rape.

Because I am in multiple ways the target of such dehumanization, I read history books with the skepticism of an incest survivor at a family gathering. I watch everyone's hands. I know the purpose of many of the stories being told is to establish the appropriateness of sacrificing me and my peoples to someone else's interests. Recovery from trauma requires creating and telling another story about the experience of violence and the nature of the participants, a story powerful enough to restore a sense of our own humanity to the abused.

~3~

Our capacity as a society to think about traumatic events and their effect on people has been disrupted by both the silencing imposed on us by perpetrators and the effects of trauma itself. The tendency is for prolonged abuse to become normalized, and even more so when it is perpetrated on a collective scale by those with the greatest power. Judith Herman looks at the checkered past of the psychological study of trauma, describing it as one of "episodic amnesia:"

> Periods of active investigation have alternated with periodic oblivion. Repeatedly in the past century, similar lines of inquiry have been taken up and abruptly abandoned, only to be rediscovered much later... This intermittent amnesia is not the result of the ordinary changes in fashion that affect any intellectual pursuit. The study of psychological trauma does not languish for lack of interest. Rather, the subject provokes such intense controversy that it periodically becomes anathema. The study of psychological trauma has repeatedly led into realms of the unthinkable and foundered on fundamental questions of belief.[3]

This is because examining psychological trauma inevitably leads us to the most widespread source of trauma, which is oppression. Therefore, it is only in the context of social movements opposing oppression that psychological trauma can really be examined. Herman argues:

> The systematic study of psychological trauma therefore depends on the support of a political movement. Indeed, whether such a study can be pursued or discussed in public is itself a political question. The study of war trauma becomes legitimate only in a context that challenges the sacrifice of young men in war. The study of trauma in sexual and domestic life becomes legitimate only in the context that challenges the subordination of women and children. Advances in the field occur only when they are supported by a political movement powerful enough to legitimate an alliance between investigators and patient and to counteract the ordinary social processes of silencing and denial. In the absence of strong political movements for human rights, the active process of bearing witness inevitably gives way to the active process of forgetting. Repression, dissociation, and denial are phenomena of social as well as individual consciousness.[4]

Denial and amnesia, repression and the dissociation that keeps our perceptions fragmented so they will not reveal the terrible whole—all of these must be overcome in order for the stories of the traumatized to occupy public space.

~4~

Healing takes place in community, in the telling and the bearing witness, in the naming of trauma and in the grief and rage and defiance that follow. In *Trauma and Recovery* Judith Herman draws from the experiences of women and men traumatized by many different kinds of events, from rape and battering to combat, from kidnaping to incest. She has found that both the effects of trauma and the recovery process from it are largely consistent across all categories of trauma. If abuse is in fact only the local manifestation of oppression, then such stages of individual recovery should also hold true for collective processes of recovery.

The significant difference, however, between a local manifestation of oppression such as incest or battering in a home and societal abuses such as racism, poverty or homophobia is the possibility of leaving the abusive situation. For individuals, recovery generally begins at the point where the abuse has been escaped or stopped. Collectively, we are often attempting to recover from abuses that are ongoing, and the only context in which recovery is possible is one of active opposition. Taking action, saying no to oppression, is an essential first step.

A stance of opposition creates a small liberated territory, a psychological space in which we can act on the belief that we deserve complete freedom and dignity even when achieving such freedom collectively is still out of reach. The refusal to cooperate with our dehumanization even when we may not yet be able to stop it increases our reserves of dignity and hope. In that moment we have begun the process of recovery—of reclaimed humanity—that is both the ultimate outcome and the most essential ingredient of our liberation. And although there is a critical role for allies in bearing witness to and taking a strong moral stance against the abuse, this activism must be by the traumatized on their own behalf.

Writing of the therapeutic relationship for traumatized individuals, Herman states that the client must be "author and arbiter of her own recovery... No intervention that takes power away from the survivor can possibly foster her recovery, no matter how much it appears to be in her immediate best interest."[5] I am reminded of a quote from an unidentified Australian aboriginal woman activist, "If you have come here to help me then you are wasting your time, but if you have come because your liberation is bound up with mine then let us work together."

What is clinically referred to as diagnosis, the naming of the problem, is the essential stage of reconnecting symptom and cause, pain and its source. Identifying the cause-and-effect relationships between nightmares and incest, depression and violation of any kind, fear and the experience of violence, releases the traumatized from the business-as-usual denial that these things can reasonably be expected to have an impact. My own relief at the discovery, in therapy, that my inability to sleep, or the persistent intrusive violent images that thrust their way into my mind were a common, known and documented response to severe abuse was identical with what I felt in my first women's consciousness-raising group. As each woman in turn spoke about her life and we recognized how much we had in common, we became able to identify the sources of our anger, frustration and self-doubt in the treatment we had recieved at the hands of men. Our exhilaration came from the realization that our pain was not after all a character flaw but a direct result of systematic injustice and that our reactions made complete sense. Oppressed communities have created many forms—from support groups to written testimony, from "speak bitterness" sessions to autobiographical anthologies—through which the connections between conditions of oppression and their impact on the oppressed can be made explicit and public. While the false memory theoreticians attempt to establish that pain is ahistoric and traumas leave no trace of themselves in our lives, the traumatized keep finding ways to insist that pain has documentable origins, that when someone is hit, it hurts, and that injuries leave scars.

Without this naming process, the effects of trauma come to seem like personal flaws or cultural defects, inborn in the traumatized, not violently created. Survivors of long-term abuse, unable to identify the external sources of self-hatred, shame, anger and fear, may pose a significant danger to themselves through direct self-harming, passive failures of self-protection, or an intense and pathological dependence on the abuser. Traumatized communities certainly enact these same behaviors. Internalizing the perpetrator's rationalizations, they may come to believe they are the source of their own problems and treat themselves and each other with disrespect and violence. Drug abuse, alcoholism, gang violence, domestic violence and a stunted sense of what is possible can all be seen as a result of the inability to identify the causes of pain and take an active stance to end them. Only when we are able to take in the cumulative impact of slavery, lynching and other forms of organized violence, enforced poverty and segregation and the systematic denial of opportunities to African Americans can we find ways to talk about the violence inflicted by young Black men upon each other as caused, not inherent.

Speaking of individual trauma patients, Herman writes:

> The question of what is wrong with them has often become hopelessly muddled and ridden with moral judgement... A conceptual framework that relates the patient's problems with identity and relationships to the trauma history provides a useful basis for the formation of a therapeutic alliance—this framework both recognizes the harmful nature of the abuse and provides a reasonable explanation for the patient's persistent difficulties.[6]

In order to establish a culture of resistance, a climate in which the oppressed are able to diagnose our own ills as the effects of oppression, we need a body of diagnostic know-how, a tradition of recognizing and understanding in detail the harmful nature of oppression.

~5~

The way we are taught our history is an endless repetition of the perpetrator's story, in which crusaders are shining knights, not massacring mercenaries, wars are glorious, conquerors noble and as far back as we can see, the past unrolls in an infinite time line of thrones, treaties and battles, and the acquisition of exciting new markets and territories. For the subjugated and colonized, the presentation of such a story as one of admirable accomplishments is an added injury. Just as the individual recovering from abuse must reconstruct the story of her undeserved suffering in a way that gives it new meaning, and herself a rebuilt and invulnerable sense of worth, the victims of collective abuse need ways to reconstruct history in a way that restores a sense of our inherent value as human beings, not simply in our usefulness to the goals of the elites.

When individuals take on such projects of recovery we often find it far more challenging than we may have expected. Herman writes, "Denial makes them feel crazy, but facing the full reality seems beyond what any human can bear."[7] The heart of the challenge is to assimilate the terrible, the unbearable, transforming it into something that can be integrated; something that can nourish us and leave us with a vision of the world, of ourselves, of humanity, that is bigger than the horror.

What is so dreadful is that to transform the traumatic we must re-enter it fully, and allow the full weight of grief to pass through our hearts. It is not possible to digest atrocity without tasting it first, without assessing on our tongues the full bitterness of it. Ours is a society that does not do grief well or easily, and what is required to face trauma is the ability to mourn, fully and deeply, all that has been taken from us. But mourning is painful and we resist giving way to it, distract ourselves with put-on toughness out of pride.

Herman talks about all the ways individuals resist mourning. Out of pride because we will not give them the satisfaction. Through fantasies of revenge rooted in a sense of helplessness, as if perpetrating abusive acts ourselves would restore our power. Through dreams of absolution in which the impact of abuse is erased by an act of love and the abuser is finally repentant. Through fantasies of compensation that allow us to avoid the truth, which is that nothing can ever compensate us.

But only through mourning everything we have lost can we discover that we have in fact survived; that our spirits are indestructible. Only through mourning can we reach a place of clean anger in which we stand with all the abused and hold the abusers accountable. Only through mourning can we reconnect to the love in our lives and lose our fascination with the ones who harmed us. And only if we fully acknowledge and grieve the hurts can we possibly find genuine compassion for the perpetrators. Mourning is the only way to honor what was lost, and only by renouncing all hope of restitution are we free to grieve.

What does grief have to do with history? Everything. In the early 1980s my mother wrote "Concepts of Pollution" about her experience studying anthropology:

Did you know Levi-Strauss wrote an essay on the pregnant boy myths
of the Pawnee Indians, myths about how some boys got supernatural
help to become doctors—so called medicine men—without a word
about doctoring among the Pawnees in the 1800's, without a word
about the desperate hopelessness of it with people dying of all the
diseases of starvation, the hungry, cold winters and the attacks of the
Sioux? ...And I was there to be a scholar, there to be an anthropologist.
Not there to be a person, a woman. Not there to care that I was Puerto
Rican, a child of Taino Indians, of Spaniards, of African slaves. Not
there to question, to argue. Not there to identify. Not there to cry.
Certainly not there to cry. No wonder I drank... I'd write after staying
up drinking, talking to myself in the mirror, shouting angrily...Then I
would write about Pawnees dying in the thin winter sunlight, coughing
up blood, or Polynesians dying on the beach in the Pacific, shot by
passing whalers, or caduveo dying of Spanish gunshot. I wrote about
Wounded Knee and Canyon de Chelly, places I had names for, and all
the beaches and valleys and rocky plains in Africa, in Canada, in
Australia, on the Pacific Islands, on the Caribbean islands, in tropical
South America, in Arctic North America, places for which I had no
names. A soundless litany of death... Drink deadens the pain, and now
I don't drink and the pain returns undeadened, unalloyed, clear and
punishing. How can I bear it? How do you mourn endless numbers of
people in endless numbers of places? Is there a form for it, a requisite
time and place for mourning? Is there ever an end to it?[8]

The only way to bear the overwhelming pain of oppression is by
telling, in all its detail, in the presence of witnesses and in a context of
resistance, how unbearable it is. If we attempt to craft resistance without
undertaking this task, we are collectively vulnerable to all the errors of
judgment that unresolved trauma generates in individuals. It is part of
our task as revolutionary people, people who want deep-rooted, radical
change, to be as whole as it is possible for us to be. This can only be done
if we face the reality of what oppression really means in our lives, not as
abstract systems subject to analysis, but as an avalanche of traumas
leaving a wake of devastation in the lives of real people who nevertheless
remain human, unquenchable, complex and full of possibility.

Radical history has the potential to do this work. Radical historians,
whether academically taught or trained in the storytelling traditions of
their communities, have the ability to do for communities of the
oppressed what a witness-bearing, morally committed therapist can do
for an individual hurt past bearing by abuse. We gather and retell the
stories of our side of history, free of the self-serving rationalizations of
the looters. In the face of every act or word that would strip us of it, we
tell, in all its anguish and beauty, the story of our ineradicable humanity.

Notes

1. Herman, Judith Lewis. *Trauma and Recovery*. Basic Books: New York, 1992, p. 8.

2. When I say the oppressed "tolerate" oppression, I am not implying that we are responsible for it. Only that although violence is an essential component of control, the primary way that elites impose their will is through threats, distortions, lies about the nature of our relationships to each other—by creating confusion among the oppressed so that we identify to some degree with the idea that these relations are normal. When large numbers of people in a society reach a point where they no longer find conditions in any way acceptable and are willing to risk whatever is required in order to change them, the threat of physical force stops being an effective control. The overthrow of Somoza happened not because the oppositon had become especially well armed or even suddenly much better organized but because large numbers of young people reached a level of outrage that overrode the habits of resignation that years of dictatorship had instilled.

3. Herman, p. 7.

4. Herman, p. 9.

5. Herman, p. 133.

6. Herman, p. 158.

7. Herman, p. 181.

8. Morales, Rosario. *Getting Home Alive*. Firebrand Books: Ithaca, New York, 1986, p. 63.

The Historian as Curandera

"Until lions write books, history will always glorify the hunter."
South African proverb

One of the first things a colonizing power or repressive regime does is attack the sense of history of those they wish to dominate by attempting to take over and control their relationships to their own past. When the invading English rounded up the harpists of Ireland and burned their harps, it was partly for their function in carrying news and expressing public opinion, for their role as opposition media; but it was also because they were repositories of collective memory. When the Mayan codices were burned, it was the Mayan sense of identity, rooted in a culture with a past, that was assaulted. The prohibitions against slaves speaking their own languages, reading and writing, playing drums, all had obvious uses in attempting to prevent organized resistance, but they were also ways of trying to control the story of who slaves thought they were.

One important way that colonial powers seek to disrupt the sense of historical identity of the colonized is by taking over the transmission of culture to the young. Native American and Australian aboriginal children were taken from their families by force and required to abandon the language, dress, customs and spirituality of their own people. Irish and Welsh children in English-controlled schools, and Puerto Rican, Mexican, Native American and Chinese children in U.S. public schools, were punished and ridiculed for speaking their home languages.

Invading the historical identities of the subjugated is one part of the task, accomplished through the destruction of records, oral traditions and cultural forms and through interfering with the education of the young. The other part is the creation of an imperial version of our lives. When a controlling elite of any kind comes to power, it requires some kind of a replacement origin myth, a story that explains the new imbalances of power as natural, inevitable and permanent, as somehow inherent to the natures of master and slave, invader and invaded, and therefore unchangeable. A substitute for the memories of the colonized. Official history is designed to make sense of oppression, to say that the oppressed are oppressed because it is their nature to be oppressed. A strong sense of their own history among the oppressed undermines the project of domination. It provides an alternative story, one in which oppression is the result of events and choices, not natural law.

Imperial histories also fulfill a vital role for those who rule. Those who dominate must justify themselves and find ways to see their own dominance as not only legitimate but the only acceptable option. So the founding fathers spoke of the need to control democracy so that only those with the experience of managing wealth would be deemed fit to hold public office; some slave holders framed the kidnapping and enslavement of West Africans as beneficial to the enslaved, as offering them the blessings of a higher state of civilization; misogynist patriarchs speak of protecting woman from her own weak nature; and the colonized everywhere are defined as in need of improvement, which only a better management of their labor and resources can offer.

In his 1976 essay "Defensa de la palabra," Uruguayan writer Eduardo Galeano wrote: "What process of change can move a people that does not know who it is, nor where it came from? If it doesn't know who it is, how can it know what it deserves to be?" The role of a socially committed historian is to use history, not so much to document the past as to restore to the dehistoricized a sense of identity and possibility. Such "medicinal" histories seek to re-establish the connections between peoples and their histories, to reveal the mechanisms of power, the steps by which their current condition of oppression was achieved through a series of decisions made by real people to dispossess them; but also to reveal the multiplicity, creativity and persistence of resistance among the oppressed.

*****

History is the story we tell ourselves about how the past explains our present, and how the ways in which we tell it are shaped by contemporary needs. When debates raged in 1992 about the quincentennial of Columbus' arrival in the Americas, what was most significant about all the voices in the controversy, the official pomp and ceremony, the outraged protests of indigenous and other colonized peoples of the Americas, and the counter-attacking official responses, is that each of these positions had something vital to say about the nature of our contemporary lives and relationships, which our conflicting interpretations of the events of 1492 simply highlighted.

All historians have points of view. All of us use some process of selection through which we choose which stories we consider important and interesting. We do history from some perspective, within some particular worldview. Storytelling is not neutral. Curandera historians make this explicit, openly naming our partisanship, our intent to influence how people think.

Between 1991 and 1996 I researched and wrote *Remedios*, a medicinal version of Puerto Rican history, told through the lives of women not so much because the pasts of Puerto Rican women were inherently important to talk about, but because I wanted to change the way Puerto Rican women think of ourselves historically. As a result, I did not attempt to write a comprehensive general history, but rather to frame historic events in ways that would contribute to decolonizing the historical identities and imaginations of Puerto Rican women and to the creation of a culture of resistance.

Remedios is testimonio, both in the sense of a life story, an autobiography of my relationship to my past, and, like the testimonios of Latin American torture survivors, in bearing witness to a much larger history of abuse and resistance in which many women and men participated. One of the most significant ways in which *Remedios* differs from conventional historical writing is in how explicitly I proclaim that my interest in history lies in its medicinal uses, in the power of history to provide those healing stories that can restore the humanity of the traumatized, and not for any inherent interest in the past for its own sake. *Remedios* does not *tell* history so much as it *interrogates* it. It seeks to be provocative rather than comprehensive, looking for potency, more than the accumulation of information.

In the writing, I chose to make myself visible not only as a historian with an agenda, but also as a subject of this history and one of the traumatized seeking to recover herself. My own work became less and less about creating a reconstructed historical record and more and more a use of my own relationship to history, my questions and challenges, my mapping of ignorance and contradiction, my anger and sorrow and exhilaration, to testify, through my personal responses to them, to how the official and renegade stories of the past impact Puerto Rican women. To explore, by sharing how I had done so in my own life, the ways that recaptured history could be used as a tool of recovery from a multitude of blows. In writing *Remedios*, I made myself the site of experimentation and engaged in a process of decolonizing my own relationship to history as one model of what was possible.

As I did so, I evolved a set of understandings or instructions to myself about how to do this kind of work, a kind of curandera's handbook of historical practice. The rest of this essay is that handbook.

1) Tell untold or undertold histories.

The first and most obvious choice is to seek out and tell those histories that have not been told or have not been told enough. If history books looked like the population of the world, they would be full of women, poor people, workers, children, people of color, slaves, the colonized. In the case of *Remedios,* where I had already chosen to tell Puerto Rican history through the lives of women, this meant continually seeking out and emphasizing the stories of women who were poor, African, indigenous, mestiza and mulatta, women enslaved and indentured, rural women, emigrant women in the United States.

2) Centering women changes the landscape.

Making truly medicinal history requires that we do more than just add women (or any other "disappeared" group of people) to the existing frameworks. We need to ask, "If women are assumed to be the most important people in this story, how will that change the questions we ask? How will it change our view of what events and processes are most important? How will it change the answers to questions that have already been asked?

For example, if you ask, "Until what point did the indigenous Arawak people of Puerto Rico have a significant impact on the society?" most Puerto Rican historians will say that the Arawaks stopped playing a major part by around 1550 because they no longer existed as a people. But what no longer existed in 1550 were organized lowland villages, caciques, war bands—in other words, those aspects of social organization that European men would consider most important and be most likely to recognize. If we ask the same question centered on women, we would need to look at those areas of life in which women had the most influence. Evidence from other parts of the Americas shows that traditional cultures survived longest in those arenas controlled by non-elite women. If we put women at the center, it may be that Arawak culture continued to have a strong influence on rural Puerto Ricans until much later, particularly in the practices of agriculture and medicine, certain kinds of spirituality, childrearing, food preparation, and in the production of cloth and pottery.

Similarly, in exploring when Puerto Ricans first began to have a distinct sense of nationality other than as Spanish colonial settlers, the usual evidence considered is the publication of newspapers or the formation of patriotic societies, activities dominated by men. How did women experience nationality? If, as José Luís Gonzalez asserts, the first people to see themselves as Puerto Rican were Black because they lacked mobility and were, perforce, committed to Puerto Rico, what about the impact of women's mobility or lack of it? Did women experience a commitment to Puerto Rican identity as a result of childbearing and extended family ties? Did they feel Puerto Rican earlier or later than men?

If women are at the center, what is the significance, what were the gains and losses of the strongly feminist Puerto Rican labor movement of the early 20th century? Medicinal history does not just look for ways to "fit in" more biographies of people from under-represented groups. It shifts the landscape of the question asked.

3) Identify strategic pieces of misinformation and contradict them.

In challenging imperial histories, some kinds of misinformation have more of an impact than others. Part of the task of a curandera historian is diagnosis. We need to ask ourselves what aspects of imperial history do the most harm, which lies are at the foundations of our colonized sense of ourselves. Some of these strategic pieces of misinformation will be the same for all projects, and I name several below. Some will be of central importance only to specific histories. In the case of Puerto Rican history, a few of the specific lies I decided were important to debunk were the absence or downplaying of Africa and African people from official histories, the idea that there was such a thing as "pure" Spanish culture in 1492 or at any time since and the invisibility of Puerto Ricans' relations with people from the other islands, especially the French, English and Dutch colonies. The first is about erasure, the other two deal with ideas of national or cultural purity.

4) Make absences visible.

The next three points deal with the nature and availability of historical evidence. When you are investigating and telling the history of disenfranchised people, you can't always find the kind and amount of written material you want. But in medicinal history the goal is as much to generate questions and show inconsistencies as it is to document people's lives.

For example, tracing absences can balance a picture, even when you are unable to fill in the blanks. Lack of evidence doesn't mean you can't name and describe what is missing. Tracing the outlines of a woman-shaped hole in the record, talking about the existence of women about whom we know only general information, can be a powerful way of correcting imperial history. I wrote one piece about the indigenous women known to have been brought to Puerto Rico from other parts of Central, South and North America who left little trace of their real names, and even less of what nations they came from.

> We are your Indian grandmothers from Eastern America, stolen from our homes and shipped to wherever they needed our work. From Tierra Firme to the islands. From one island to another. From this side to that, each colony raiding for its own supply... They have passenger lists with the names of those who came west over the ocean to take our lands, but our names are not recorded... Some of us died so far from home we couldn't even imagine the way back: Cherokee in Italy, Tupi in Portugal, Inuit in Denmark. Many of us were fed into the insatiable gold mines of el imperio alongside the people of your island, and they called us simply indias. But we were as different from one another as Kongo from Wolof, Italian from Dane...We are the ancestors of whom no record has been kept. We are trace elements in your bodies, minerals coloring your eyes, residue in your fingernails. You were not named for us. You don't know the places where our bones are, but we are in your bones. Because of us, you have relatives among the many tribes. You have cousins on the reservations...

It is also possible to use fictitious characters to highlight an absence, as Virginia Woolf does in *A Room of One's Own* when she speaks of Shakespeare's talented and fictitious sister, for whom no opportunities were open. I wrote a similar piece about the invented sister of a Spanish chronicler who visited Puerto Rico in the 18th century to make visible the absence of women chroniclers.

5) Asking questions can be as good as answering them.

Another way of dealing with lost history is to ask speculative questions. "What if?" is a legitimate tool of investigation, and the question can be as valuable as an answer. Proposing a radically different interpretation is a way of opening up how we think about events, even when there is no way to prove anything. It is useful to ask, "What would have to be different for us to understand this story in this other way?"

The chronicles of the Spanish conquest of Puerto Rico have relatively little to say about the cacica Guanina and her liaison with the Spaniard Cristóbal Sotomayor. The popularized version I grew up on goes something like this. Innocent Indian maiden sees the most handsome man she's ever laid eyes on, far surpassing anyone in her whole culture. She falls in love with him, even though he has enslaved her community, who are dying like flies. She becomes his lover, and when her people plot an uprising, she runs to warn him. He doesn't take her seriously, not because he's arrogant, but because he's brave, and promptly rides into an ambush and dies. Guanina is beside herself with grief. Her brother the chief finds her dead body lying across her slain lover, the two are buried side by side and the lilies of Spain entwine with the wildflowers of Puerto Rico upon their graves.

On the face of it, this is an extremely unlikely tale. Guanina was the niece of the high cacique of Puerto Rico, in a matrilineal society in which sisters' children inherited. At eighteen she would have been considered a full adult, and a woman of influence and prestige. Puerto Rico, called Boriken by the Arawaks, was not settled by European colonists until 1508. By the time Guanina and Sotomayor are known to have been lovers, the Arawaks of Boriken on the eve of the 1511 uprising had had eighteen years of news from Hispaniola and had a pretty good idea of what was likely to happen to them. Beth Brant, writing on Pocahontas, argues that indigenous women sometimes sought out liaisons with European men as a way of creating ties of kinship, in the hope that such a bond would help them fend off the worst consequences of invasion. If all we do is assume, for a moment, that Guanina was not naive, but was an intelligent woman, used to seeing herself as important, and that she was thinking about what she was doing, the colonialist story becomes completely implausible. My reinterpretation of Guanina's story is based on that implausibility and simply proposes another possible set of motives and understandings that could explain the known facts of her life and death and leave us with a sense of her dignity and purpose. It is speculative, and without hard evidence, but it opens up important questions about how to understand the actions of smart people in intolerable conditions.

6) What constitutes evidence?

Another issue to keep in mind is the bias built into historical standards of evidence. Although there is an increasing acceptance of other forms of documentation, the reliance is still heavily on the written. Which means that we accept an immense body of experience as unavailable for historical discussion. The fact that something was written down does not make it true, as any critical consumer of the media knows. It simply means that someone with sufficient authority to write things down recorded their version of events or transactions while someone else did not. It is evidence of some of what they did, some of what they wanted others to think they did and some of what they thought about it. No more. Of course even something as partial as this is a treasure trove, but when we rely on written records we need to continually ask ourselves what might be missing, what might have been recorded in order to manipulate events and in what direction, and in what ways we are allowing ourselves to assume that objectivity is in any way connected with literacy. We need to remind ourselves that much of what we want to know wasn't written about, and also think about ways to expand what we will consider as contributing to evidence. Is the oral tradition of a small town, handed down over fourteen generations, about the mass exodus of local men to the gold mines of Brazil, really less reliable than what women tobacco workers charged with civil offenses deposed before a judge whose relatives owned tobacco fields? As historians of the under-represented, we need to question the invalidation of non-literate mechanisms of memory.

7) Show agency.

One of the big lies of imperial history is that only members of the elite act, and everyone else is acted upon. In our attempts to expose the cruelty of oppression, we sometimes portray oppressed communities as nothing more than victims and are unable to see the full range of responses that people always make to their circumstances. People who are being mistreated are always trying to figure out a strategy. Those strategies may be shortsighted, opportunistic, ineffective or involve the betrayal of others, but they nevertheless represent a form of resistance. Politically, it's essential that we learn to develop strategies that hold out for real transformation whenever possible and that take everyone's well-being into account. But in telling the history of our struggles with each other over time, it's important to recognize that resistance takes many forms. We need to dismantle the idea of passive victimization, which leaves us feeling ashamed and undeserving of freedom. Even under the most brutal conditions, people find ways to assert their humanity. Medicinal history must find ways to show the continual exercise of choice by people who appear powerless.

8) Show complexity and embrace ambiguity and contradiction.

In order to do this, we must also give up the idea that people are 100 percent heroic or villainous. In searching out a history of resistance, the temptation is to find heroic figures and either overlook their failings or feel betrayed when we find that they have some. Human beings are not all resistance or collaboration and complicity. Popular imperial history tends to be ahistorical and simplistic, focused on exceptional personalities instead of complex social processes. If we ignore what is contradictory about our own impulses toward solidarity or betrayal in an attempt to simplify history into good and evil, we will sacrifice some of the most important lessons to be gained.

We need more than just the heroic stories of militant resistance. Stories of accommodation, collaboration and outright defeat are just as important because they give us ways to understand our position as caused rather than just existing. If we want to give people a sense of agency, of having always been actors as well as acted upon, we must be willing to tell stories full of contradiction that show the real complexity of the causes of their current conditions.

For example, Nzinga, born in 1585, was a queen among the Mbundu of what is now Angola. She was a fierce anti-colonial warrior, a militant fighter, a woman holding power in a male-dominated society, and she laid the basis for successful Angolan resistance to Portuguese colonialism all the way into the 20th century. She was also an elite woman living from the labor of others, murdered her brother and his children, fought other African people on behalf of the Portuguese and collaborated in the slave trade.

I tell her story· in two different ways, once at the end of her life, celebrating her anti-colonial militancy and the power of her memory for Black women, and once from the point of view of the woman on whose back she literally sat as she negotiated with the Portuguese governor. It is in many ways more empowering when we show our heroic figures as contradictory characters full of weaknesses and failures of insight. Looking at those contradicitons enables us to see our own choices more clearly and to understand that imperfect people can have a powerful, liberating impact on the world.

9) Reveal hidden power relationships.

Imperial history obscures the power relations that underlie our daily lives. This is one of the ways that immense imbalances of power and resources are made to seem natural. In telling the history of an oppressed community, we need to expose those relationships of unequal power whether they come from outside our group or lie within it. Puerto Rican liberal feminists of the late 19th century, all those "firsts" in the arts and education, came primarily from an hacendado class made affluent by the slave-produced profits of the sugar industry. Many of the leaders of the 1868 Lares uprising against Spain were coffee planters angered by their growing dependence on newly arrived merchants and the credit they offered.

Another way to expose unequal power is to reveal hidden economic relationships. I did this in part by following the products of Puerto Rican women's labor to their destinations and tracing the objects of their daily use to their sources. This both shows the degree of control exerted on our lives by the profit-seeking of the wealthy and uncovers relationships we have with working people in other parts of the world. In the 1600s ginger grown by Puerto Rican women and men was sold to English smugglers from Jamaica and ended up spicing the daily gingerbread of London's working poor. One of the main items imported in exchange was used clothing made in the mills of England and the Low Countries. This reveals a different relationship between Puerto Ricans and English people than the "great civilization/ insignificant primitive colony" story told in the 1923 *Encyclopaedia Britannica* we had in my home, which described Puerto Rico as a small island with no natural resources. Telling Puerto Rican community college students that the stagehands for Shakespeare's productions probably ate Puerto Rican food on their lunch breaks changes their relationship to that body of "high culture."

Similarly, Puerto Rican women and children picked and processed coffee that was considered the best in the world at the turn of the century. Yauco coffee was served in the wealthiest homes of New York, Paris and Vienna. Mrs. J.P. Morgan bought her personal supply from Yauco, and all those philosophers, poets and painters drank it at their salons. Juxtaposing photographs of coffee workers who earned pennies for their labor with the silver coffeepots and reclining gentry who consumed the coffee restores Puerto Rican women's labor to its place in an international web of trade and profit.

I wrote one piece in which I described the lunch preparations of a rural Puerto Rican neighbor and showed how the food she set on the table was a map of the world, showing her connections to people in Malaysia, Ethiopia, Portugal and many other places. I described the vegetables grown and canned in the Imperial and Salinas Valleys of California by Mexican and Filipina women and promoted as the "modern" replacement for fresh produce to Puerto Rican housewives of the late '40s and '50s. I read this piece as part of a talk I gave at a small college in Michigan, including a section about bacalao, the dry salt cod that is a staple protein of Puerto Rican cuisine.

> The bacalao is the fin-tip of a vast movement in which the shadows of small fishing boats skim across the Grand Banks of Nova Scotia hauling cod from immense schools of feeding fish, salt it down in their holds and return with rumors of great lands to fourteenth-century Basque fishing villages and Portuguese port towns. Return to Iceland, to New Brunswick and Nova Scotia, to build up the great shipping fortunes of Massachusetts. The flaking yellow flesh makes her part of a wide Atlantic net of people who live from the cod: catch the cod, salt the

cod, pack and ship the cod, sell the cod, import and export the cod, stretch a piece of it into food for a family for a week.

After the talk, a man came up to me, deeply moved, to tell me that he had grown up in a Nova Scotia fishing village and his family had packed cod. I thanked him and told him we had eaten it for breakfast. "So did we!" he exclaimed. "We ate it with green bananas," I told him. "We ate it with potatoes," he replied, and we embraced. The last place he had expected to hear about his own life was in a talk on Puerto Rican women's history. Revealing this kind of connection increases a sense of our common interests and uncovers the importance of our labor in the international scheme of things.

10) Personalize.

The majority of historical figures who are known by name are members of elite groups, while everyone else tends to be known en masse. However, there are quite a few places where the names of individual people who are poor, female, dark, etc., can be found in written records. Using the names of individual real people, and any details we know about their lives, to dramatize and personalize the social condition of a group makes those conditions far more real. When the disenfranchised appear only in crowd scenes, it reinforces a sense of relative unimportance.

In writing about the lives of recently freed slave women in Puerto Rico, I used names of real women found in a footnote in a book on slavery in San Juan that contained the details of what family members they sought out after emancipation and what work they did. This has an entirely different impact than writing, "many freed women sought out their relatives and contracted to work for them."

The best-documented Arawak women are cacicas, members of the indigenous ruling class known as nitainos. Most of the stories about Arawak women focus on cacicas like Guanina, Loiza or Anacaona. But we know that the majority of Arawak women belonged to the naboría laborer class. I found a list of indigenous women both from Boriken and from the smaller islands of the Eastern Caribbean who were being branded as slaves on one particular day in 1515. Many were given two names in the record, one Spanish and one Arawak or Carib and many others simply renamed Maria or Catalina. By using names that were at least imposed on real women, and the few facts recorded about them, their anonymity in the imperial records is at least made visible and the realities of their lives during the conquest become more tangible. Here is an example from my poem "1515: Naborías:"

They were not cacicas.
They were not heirs to yuca fields.
There were no concessions made to their status.
They were not "queens."

Their names are recorded in the lists of work gangs
sent to the mines, the conucos, the kitchens, the laundries
of the Spanish invaders.
> Macaney, field hand.
> Francisquilla, cook.
> Ana, baker.
> Catalina, pig woman.

They were the working women of Boriken.
They were called out of their names.
Casually recorded under the names of Catholic saints,
or the queens of the myriad kingdoms of Spain, renamed
after little sisters or mothers left behind in Estremadura,
Navarra, Castilla, Sevilla, León
or a favorite prostitute from a port town,
or a beauty out of some ballad of the old land.
They were not born Catalina, Ana, Francisquilla...

The account books of the governor say *herrose*—
branded on this day— was Elvira Arumaita
from the island of Guadalupe
with a son they called Juaníco.
herrose, a Carib called Beatríz, and her son, Juaníco.
herrose, a Carib, Juana Cabarotaxa, from the island of Santa Cruz,
    and
herrose, a little girl called Anita, Carib,
from the aforementioned island
which we now call Guadalupe, and *herrose,*
also from Guadalupe, Magdalena Guavrama
Carib, and her child.

They were already here, enslaved, escaped,
and to their great misfortune, recaptured
and branded this day by Captain Juan Ponce de León,
> Ana Taguas, Violante Ateyba
> Leonor Yayguana written down as belonging
> to the rebel cacique Abey,
> and Isabel Guayuca with her son, once again Juaníco,
> once owing loyalty to the collaborator Cayey.
They were women under two masters,
the crumbling authority of the caciques

and the new and violent usage of the señores...

In cases where we really don't have names, documented elements in the lives of a social group can still be personalized by writing a personal narrative that conveys the reality of such a life. I used figures on average wages of women working in coffee, sugar and garment work in the early 20th century along with a list of the prices of housing and essential foods to write an internal monologue about the kinds of choices a single mother of several children has to make during the dead season of the sugar cane industry when there is little work and a lot of illness. Details like the difference between feeding your children unbroken rice, broken rice or cornmeal make the actual struggles of such women visible and felt in a way that lists of numbers alone cannot.

11) Show connection and context.

One element of imperial history is that events tend to be seen as caused by extraordinary personalities acting on one another without showing us the social context. For example, many of the great discoveries and inventions we are taught about in elementary and high school were being pursued by many people at once, but the individual who received the patent is described as a lone explorer rather than part of a group effort. Rosa Parks didn't "get tired" one day and start the Montgomery bus boycott. She was a trained organizer, and her role, as well as the time and place of the boycott, was the result of careful planning by a group of civil rights activists. Just as medicinal history must restore individuality to anonymous masses of people, it must also restore social context to individuals singled out as the actors of history.

12) Restore global context.

One element of imperial history that is particularly strong in the United States is a sense that the rest of the world is irrelevant. Few U.S. residents are knowledgeable about the geography, politics, culture and history of other countries. In 1968, when I was fourteen, I spent a summer in Cuba. One of the most striking things for me was opening the paper each day to find regular ongoing coverage of dozens of countries I had only heard of before as occasional "hot spots" or tourist destinations. Imperial history tends to talk about the world outside of imperial headquarters episodically, as if it existed only when the attention of the empire was upon it.

The way I was taught ancient history left me with an impression of a darkened world in which nothing happened until the lights of civilization were turned on, first in Mesopotamia, then in Ancient Greece, then

Rome, then spreading northwestward into Europe. Only then, as European expansion took off, did the Americas, Asia and Africa appear. It was at home, from my father, that I learned of Chinese merchants trading with East Africa in the 12th century, or the vast expanse and intellectual achievements of the Islamic empire.

One of the tasks, therefore, of medicinal history is to show that all parts of the world coexist and always have. (Contrary to popular expressions like "Stone Age people" or "just entering the 20th century," all people now alive are living at the same time, whatever our technologies or forms of social organization.) We also need to show that complexity and change exist and always have existed in all parts of the world.

One of my current projects is a curriculum that starts from Shakespeare's England and connects his life and writings to events and people in the rest of the world. How many of us are ever asked to think about what was happening in China, Peru and Mali while *Hamlet* was being written? In my Puerto Rican history project, I included an ancient and a medieval section in which I showed the diversity and vitality of people's lives in the three regions from which Puerto Ricans originate: West Africa, the Mediterranean and the Caribbean. I wanted to create a sense of balance among the regions long before 1492.

As a discipline, history is taught by regions and time periods, in ways that often make it difficult to focus on linkages. Medicinal history can restore a sense of the global to fragmented colonial histories. The arrival of the Spanish in the Caribbean is closely connected with the expulsions of Jews and Moslems from Spain, linking the history of San Juan with that of Constantinople and Marrakech. The upheavals that the slave trade brought to West Africa, and the conflicts among and within African nations have a direct bearing on who showed up in the slave markets of the island. The fact that General Nelson Miles, who led the U.S. invasion of Puerto Rico in 1898, was also the most prominent military commander of the wars against the Plains Indians is not just biographical information about Miles' career. It connects the stories of peoples affected by U.S. expansion from Puerto Rico to the Dakotas, from Idaho and Arizona to Hawaii and the Philippines. Re-establishing a sense of the connectedness of world events is a critical piece of the work of the activist historian.

13) Access and Digestibility.

If the purpose of medicinal history is to transform the way we see ourselves historically, to change our sense of what's possible, then making history available to those who need it most is not a separate process from the researching and interpreting. The task of the curandera historian includes delivery.

To do exciting, empowering research and leave it in academic journals and university libraries is like manufacturing unaffordable medicines for deadly diseases. We need to share our work in ways that people can assimilate, not in the private languages and forms of scholars. This is the difference between curanderas and pharmaceutical companies. Pharmaceuticals are going into indigenous and other people-of-color communities worldwide to steal and patent traditional science, technology and even the plants themselves and produce medicines that are completely out of reach of the people who invented them. We need to be careful, in doing historical research about oppressed communities, to see that the active ingredients get back to the people whose ancestors generated our work.

A good medicine also includes a delivery system, something that gets it to the parts of your body that need it. Those who are hungriest for what we dig up don't read scholarly journals and shouldn't have to. As historians we need to either be artists and community educators or find people who are and figure out how to collaborate with them. We can work with community groups to create original public history projects that really involve people. We can see to it that our work gets into at least the local popular culture through theater, murals, historical novels, posters, films, children's books or a hundred other art forms. We can work with elementary and high-school teachers to create curricula. Medicinal history is a form of healing and its purposes are conscious and overt.

14) Show yourself in your work.

One of the pretenses of history is that being rigorous about research is the same as being objective. Since history is a collection of stories about people in conflict, and all our families were involved, it seems a ridiculous claim. Objectivity isn't all it's cracked up to be anyway. Being objective is often understood to mean not taking sides; but failing to take sides when someone is being hurt is immoral. In writing about the past, we are choosing to bear witness to the impact of that past on the people around us. We don't stand apart from history. We are in the midst of it right this minute and the stances we take matter. A committed moral stance does not mean that we cannot be rigorous. While the agenda of the activist historian is to rescue a sense of worth for the oppressed, our ability to see worth in the contradictory and ambiguous means we welcome the full picture. We don't, in the narrow sense, have an axe to grind.

Part of what oppression tries to teach us is that as intellectuals we need not involve ourselves and that it is undignified to do so. Certainly to talk and write openly about our personal, emotional and intellectual stakes in our work is frowned on, and lets us in for ridicule and disrespect. Nevertheless, it's important for people's historians not to hide ourselves. Part of what keeps our work honest is acknowledging why we care about it and who we are in relationship to it. We often write the books we most need to read, and do research that in some way touches on core issues in our lives. Revealing this is a way of shedding the cloak of apartness and revealing our humanity.

15) Cross borders

At a lecture I gave on my historical research, someone asked how I found all these myriad connections between seemingly unrelated topics. I realized, as I answered her, that the key thing had been allowing myself to be widely curious, across all boundaries of discipline, geography and time. Academic training and the workings of the higher education marketplace exert powerful pressures on us to narrow our interests and not cross into unfamiliar territory. A commitment to the study of connections requires us to continually do so. The categories of discipline, geography and historical period are themselves constructed in obedience to certain priorities that don't necessarily serve the projects of medicinal history. Borders are generally established in order to exercise control, and when we center our attention of the historical empowerment of the oppressed, we inevitably swim rivers, lift barbed wire and violate "no trespassing" signs.

The Tribe of Guarayamín

"The master's tools will never dismantle the master's house."

Audre Lorde

Leaving the Master's House

One of the results of prolonged oppression is that our vision becomes polarized into the two possibilities of the abused and the abuser, so that sometimes the only picture of liberation we can form is to sit on the same throne we have been forced to kneel before, to take possession of the castle without stopping to examine whether it is in fact fit for human habitation. Sometimes when we're trying the hardest to restore a sense of our place in history, we get seduced into trying yet again to show that our people meet the crooked standards of excellence of the conquistadores and slave holders. Reactive history is still in the grip of imperial thinking and it always sacrifices someone to imperial dreams.

Feminist history that holds up as models queens who were imperious and forceful in their own right and ruthlessly exploited the peasantry they ruled over. Afrocentric scholars who, in order to restore dignity to the formerly enslaved, glorify kingdoms and empires built on war and conquest, and attribute the varied and sophisticated accomplishments of Mexican, Central American and Andean civilizations to small but incredibly influential groups of visitors from Mali, Phoenicia and Egypt, doing to the people of the Americas exactly what Eurocentric scholars have done with Africa. Versions of Mexican history that glorify Aztec society, which believed that the sun must be raised each morning by the spirits of young warriors tortured and sacrificed, only to be dragged into darkness each night by the spirits of women who died in childbirth; or pretend that the empire had no downside for the surrounding peoples.

These versions of history collaborate with the myths of our separateness, our lack of accountability to each other, with notions of cultural purity and isolation.

They also collaborate at an even deeper level with corrupt ideas of what it means for a culture to be admirable. The capacity to dominate one's neighbors, kill them, enslave them, loot them and extract tribute from them; the ability to keep enforcing upon the population a series of bosses from the same families who accumulate wealth faster than anyone else; the construction, with stolen wealth and forced labor, of large buildings, roads, bridges, and ornate tombs and temples—this is called civilization and held up for admiration. This is the hunter glorifying the hunt.

But medicinal history doesn't want to recycle that mythology. We're not looking to put new personnel in the same old job descriptions. We need to examine carefully what aspects of our history we offer our communities as sources of pride. It is a well-documented aspect of captivity and abuse that we sometimes come to long for the approval of our captors, even when we act defiant. When being fully respected doesn't appear to be an option, and we are under the full weight of other people's greedy disregard for us, domination can look downright charismatic. It's so easy to get sucked into envy instead of righteous anger; to watch "Lifestyles of the Rich and Famous" instead of looking at how the rich and famous make decisions every day that lead directly to suffering. Rebel history has to consciously and persistently undermine the pull of the abused to admire and mimic the abusers.

Instead, we need to look for what is actually useful to us in the road our ancestors have traveled; to really stand on their shoulders. In *Africa in History,* Basil Davidson concludes a section on the emerging medieval kingdoms of West Africa by pointing out that this emphasis is deceptive: what West Africa should really be famous for is the sophistication of its social organization at the local level, the democracy of village life, and those societies that grew better at balance instead of domination. Pursuing this notion in *Remedios,* I wrote the following piece for my own section on the West African roots of Puerto Rican society.

> Those who have lived too long in the shadows of empire look only for kings and monuments and pass the villages by. They run after glittering stories of Greater Ghana, Mali and Songhay, of manikongos and sunnis, of Mansa Musa and Sundiata and the lords of Benin. There they will find the familiar power struggles of dynasties and war parties, conquests and looting. But we will step off that path and take a walk among the small societies, where Africa is born again each season and balance is found again and again.

Kingship is a blunt and clumsy tool compared to the intricate and flexible life of the villages. Power does not pile up at the top where it can topple and fall in ruins. Power falls like seed planted in a field. Each head of a family, each leader of a clan has no more than can be held in two hands and scatters it no farther than it can be thrown in a single gesture. Each village runs its own affairs but no neighboring village stands alone. The people of the small societies make patterns of loyalty and mutual obligation, as elaborate and elegant as the regalia of royalty, and of far more practical use.

The Tale of Guarayamín

Over the past few years, several different and competing groups have emerged in the U.S. Puerto Rican community claiming to be the Taíno Nation, legitimate heirs to the Arawak people who lived throughout the northwestern Caribbean islands. I began receiving e-mail communiques from the different groups, each claiming to be the real Taínos. This phenomenon has received a lot of attention and provoked considerable heated discussion in the Puerto Rican community. Debate is polarized into two equally rigid positions. Position one, the official academic version, says the Arawaks disappeared with little or no trace by 1550, have had no ongoing impact on Puerto Rican culture and any views to the contrary are romantic wishful thinking. Position two, that of the various Taíno nations, says, "We are the real Arawaks, who have survived all attempts to exterminate us and anyone who says we aren't is collaborating with a centuries-long tradition of genocide." It is strongly implied that creating tribal affiliation for the Puerto Rican descendants of the Arawaks bestows more authenticity and legitimacy on them than the complexities of mixed heritage do.

On the one hand, it is certainly true that the repartimientos that scattered Arawak villages into forced labor and divided up the limited amount of farmland among the Spanish invaders, pandemics of European diseases, and the introduction of large numbers of slaves from other parts of America as well as kidnapped Africans from many nations—all led to a widespread disintegration of organized Arawak communities and traditional social structures by the mid-16th century. The only records of Arawak culture available to us are filtered through the interpretations of Spanish priests and chroniclers who reported the conquest, or those of more recent anthropologists, archeologists and linguists poring over fragments of language and pottery.

On the other hand, it is a long-standing colonial practice to declare people extinct for a range of reasons, none of them benevolent. The survival of a culture isn't a simple yes-no proposition. As invaded people

try to cope with conquest, they try a lot of different things, accommo-
dating, resisting, fleeing, blending; and they survive in some ways and
not in others. The assumption that Arawak influence died a complete
death in 1550 certainly needs to be reconsidered. The presence or
absence of the Arawak people has been politically manipulated from the
beginning of colonialism on the island. The place I grew up in, called
Indiera, registered a population of nearly 2,000 people who called
themselves "indios" in 1797, the last year in which that category was
included in the census. As a child, I certainly saw people with strongly
indigenous features, referred to by others as indios. It is a legitimate part
of our task to ask in what ways Arawak people and cultural know-how
may have escaped the notice of biased observers.

But why reconstitute one portion of our heritage as a tribe, and why
now? Rooted in an idealized "pure" past, the creation of a small but
noble nation reenacting a memory of sovereignty is in a limited way
medicinal. In a time of deteriorating conditions, both economic and
political, with our communities living under attack in a climate of
contempt, to declare ourselves the doggedly surviving remnants of a
people said to have been wiped out centuries ago is a kind of defiant
declaration.

But it is a flawed defiance. For one thing, the authority it generates
is for a small group of men who have chosen themselves—an infinitely
useful authority since there is no intact lineage of knowledge or reliable
written record to contradict whatever the new caciques decide to do or
say. As is often the case with groups based in nationalist pride and a
vision of the past, the new tribes appear to be strongly male-dominated
and hierarchical. Their reconstruction has made them all into caciques.

But more importantly, it is built on a lie about who we are. It turns
its back on the real survival our ancestors engineered, the ingenuity of
combined wits and intricate relationships. The attempt to portray
themselves as "pure" Arawaks, in spirit if not in actuality, after five
centuries of unrestrained intermixture, is a rejection of our strong African
roots. It erases the many thousands of indigenous people brought to our
island from all the coasts of the Caribbean and the Gulf of Mexico, who
blended early on with the Arawak survivors of the encomienda. And it
rejects the presence in all of us of the Spanish immigrants, most of them
peasants, the French and Italian farmers and peddlers, who also lived on
yucca up in the hills. Instead, this story relies on an almost mystical
notion of an Arawak "essence" that can guide us through the violence
and poverty inflicted on our communities, back to a golden age of

rulership, rather than forward in multicultural alliance to a just contemporary society.

In a climate of intensifying racism, it has great appeal, especially to young U.S. Puerto Ricans seeking a source of uncomplicated pride, and the racist romanticism of U.S. society toward Native Americans makes Arawak identity seem uncomplicated. But complexity is the ground of real possibility for us.

When my brother and I first heard of this phenomenon in communiques signed by lists of men with brand-new Arawak names, we began inventing some for ourselves, words with multilingual sounds and meanings that had us rolling with laughter in the unrepentant mestiza's irreverent defiance of blood categories. We called ourselves Yaveriguaré (I'll soon find out) and Casimorí (I almost died), Yamefuí (I already left) and my personal favorite, the indignant inquiry "Guarayamín?"

We intended no disrespect toward the culture of the Arawak ancestors we also share, nor of the people who are no doubt sincere in reaching for what is to be gained from nation-making. Our laughter was that particular biting humor born from the experience of being completely misrepresented: we are the mixed among the mixed, children of a Puerto Rican mother and a Russian Jewish father, and concepts of ethnic purity have weighed on us from childhood. But it is also a laughter born from trust in the versatility of our people, our capacity to invent and reinvent ourselves in the face of every attempt to shame us.

However tempting the apparent security of a simplistic heritage may be, however addictive the lottery player's dream of moving to the penthouse, however compelling the urge to prove ourselves with rosters of warriors and kings, what our ancestors have bequeathed us is of far greater value. Our worth as a people has never rested with caciques or señores. Our beauty is not in any one strand of our inheritance, but in the rich weave of contradictory traits that a long history of struggling next to and with each other has left us: Our stubborn capacity to survive, our wicked humor at the expense of the powerful, our ability to use anything and everything we find, our gift for enjoyment.

There's a question, full of commentary, that the skeptical have often used when faced with assertions by the pretentious, of "pure" Spanish or at least European ancestry: "Y tu abuela, ¿donde está?" ("And your grandmother—where is she?") An assertion by the dark and poor that we have been mingling too long for that sort of nonsense, and if all your grandmothers were here, you couldn't get away with this obvious lie.

The real stories we need to be telling and asking about are the ones that include all those grandmothers, dark and light and in between. In them we will find the courage to abandon the false security of the master's house with its centuries-thick foundation of lies and embrace the shifting, dynamic, uncertain and contradictory realities we have inherited. Because mythologizing our pasts in the image of the master's present, as if the sum of our yearning were to occupy his place, is an injury to the authentically free future we want for our children, for our peoples, for the world.

Nightflying

Transforming Traumatic Memory

One of the challenges of effective activism is learning to simultaneously hold a clear picture of radical transformation and take advantage of the smaller opportunities that present themselves without being distracted or seduced into thinking them adequate. Reforms make life easier but don't resolve the fundamental injustices. It is tempting, easy and to some degree reasonable to seek individual remedies for oppression or become committed to fighting for a greater number of available individual remedies. Finding ways to ease the burdens of oppression is a perfectly acceptable tactic, if the real goal of eliminating it completely is kept in sight.

But to keep in mind the necessity of eliminating a whole system of injustices, we need to keep the pain, the trauma, the suffering and outrage in mind, too, and without adequate political support, it is extremely difficult to hold the reality of oppression in our awareness. Among my feminist friends who are in heterosexual relationships, all of us have a clear understanding of the scope and violence of patriarchy, but in daily life, it's much easier to keep our attention on "fixing" our male partners or negotiating small shifts of power around household chores or emotional work than to confront the reality that changing our partners' habits will not have any effect on our real position in the world. It may simply make it slightly easier to tolerate. Patriarchy can't be solved by an improvement in the communication skills or household habits of the men in our lives.

Only when there is adequate political support can we create a context in which we are able to hold the reality of oppression and a sense of our own power to oppose it. When that support doesn't exist, we avoid whatever events—in our own lives, in the lives of others or in our history—would lead us to intolerable truths.

In her book *Witchcraze*, Ann Barstow documents the inability of historians of the witch persecutions to name, in their analyses, the central importance of gender. For Barstow, this is obvious in the demographics of the victims, in the extremity of violence being inflicted by men upon women and in the overtly sexual nature of that violence. But even among feminist historians, relatively little attention has been paid to the witch trials. While there have been cultural responses to the history of the persecutions—including a reclaiming or reconstruction of various versions of European paganism, attempts to reclaim the intellectual heritage of women herbalists, midwives and healers and redeem the title of witch—and some attempts to express grief and anger over the invisibility of these events by dramatizing them, still there has been remarkably little systematic research done on what were, after all, crushing events for European women and women in some European colonies.

A thorough examination of the witch craze would force us to face the depth and intensity of misogyny and sexual violence that are bedrock in European and European-based societies. Violent upsurges of persecution like this one always have multiple causes, but what is most frightening is that they reveal the instability, the precariousness of our compromises and reforms. It is difficult to study such events honestly. They provoke shame, horror, denial and a whole range of strategies to make the intolerable bearable by minimizing either the extent of the trauma or the ways in which its roots remain intact once the eruption has subsided. Lacking a strong political movement by the traumatized to force its examination, traumatic history must either be contained and sanitized, or else it will quickly become too controversial and the most honest appraisals of its impact will be silenced.

Whether it is the transatlantic enslavement of West African peoples and the horrors of their centuries-long captivity; the ruthless genocidal warfare against indigenous peoples in the Americas; the systematic extermination of Jews, Gypsies, the disabled and other groups by the Nazis; the incineration and irradiation of the populations of Hiroshima and Nagasaki; or the arrest, sexual torture and execution of European women accused of witchcraft, the challenges are in many ways the same. We cannot bear to look because of the frightening truths these events open up about our relationships with each other in the present.

Which events we will be unable to bear examining, and which aspects of these events we will be willing to look at closely, will depend on the degree of political pressure being exerted by the traumatized, but also on how closely we identify with the victims and/or perpetrators, the current social standing of the victim group, and what continuing stakes are involved in protecting the perpetrators from accountability. For example, the great extent to which the prosperity of the Swiss economy is based on riches accumulated through collaboration with Nazi Germany and the appropriation of Jewish bank accounts gives Swiss bankers and other members of the Swiss elite a strong stake in denying many portions of documented Holocaust history. Considerable pressure had to be brought to bear directly on the profit-making abilities of the Swiss banks, pressure generated by Jews who were themselves wealthy and influential within the world of international banking, before there was any acknowledgment that Swiss bankers and lawyers had stolen hundreds of millions of dollars from Jewish depositors. The origins of Swiss affluence have been normalized and business as usual depends on that normalization.

Violence against women, contempt for women's intellectual lives, the devaluing of women's work, and fear of both our sexuality and our spirituality are so historically pervasive that they have been, to a large degree, normalized. It is easier to study the political, religious and juridical details of the witch persecutions than to ask what relationship such violence, contempt and fear had to the mass killings. What would it mean to the study of early modern European history if the witch persecutions were taught as one of the major power shifts of that precarious time? What would it mean to teach the witch trials with as much attention, inadequate though it is, as is given to the Holocaust or the African slave trade? Why is it that the witch trials tend to be seen as archaic, without contemporary relevance?

The height of the witch hunts, from the mid-1500s to the 1700s, coincided with European expansion into Africa, the Americas and Asia, and with profound economic changes within European society. Among these was the increased privatization of the natural world into property for the wealthy. In *Biopiracy,* Vandana Shiva writes about the current seizure and patenting by multinational corporations of traditional biological resources and knowledge as the enclosure of the biological and intellectual commons. The systematic persecutions of European peasant women may have been an earlier stage of the same process, for the herbalists and midwives and practitioners of folk religions had a relationship with the natural world that would have interfered with the growing monopolization of resources both inside and outside Europe, by elite European men. It was a relationship of reciprocity, of respect, of participation. That relationship had to be broken and for several hundred years the women who conveyed the common lore demonized, tormented and violently put to death to destroy their authority. Among other things, the witch persecutions established elite male monopolies of knowledge, especially medical and spiritual knowledge.

They also helped to shape policies toward the spiritual and scientific expertise of new colonial subjects in the Americas, Africa and Asia. Definitions of witchcraft expanded to embrace whole cultures, so that the Inquisitors in Cartagena de Indias in Colombia asked to be excused from prosecuting various kinds of common sorcery because, they said, they would have to arrest nearly the entire population. We need to understand more about the politics of witch hunting and its relationship to other forms of state terror, to the shaping of colonial policy, and to the structures of patriarchal power. It is as important to understand what allowed the persecutions to die away as to know what forces brought them on.

We also need to understand more about the legacy of that trauma and its continuing coercive effects on contemporary women. Fundamentalists in the South have accused pro-choice activists, especially lesbians, of using aborted fetuses in witchcraft rituals. A progressive woman labor leader in Sweden was recently accused of bewitching her opponents. In contemporary U.S. and European society, accusations of witchery do not carry enough weight to bring on mass persecutions. Any similar attack on women would frame our threat to elite male civilization in more contemporary terms.

Nevertheless, the imagery and folklore of the persecutions are strongly present in our culture, and the trauma of a campaign that left whole villages without a single living woman remains unhealed. Popular culture continually reinforces the image of the dangerous old woman dressed in dark peasant clothing and a medieval peaked hat who wants to kidnap, torment and eat children, while the few "good witches" are invariably young, beautiful and richly dressed. We are taught to fear women elders, and "witch" is still an epithet of contempt for a strong-minded assertive woman. These cultural images may not in themselves represent a threat, but they are the residue of a time in which women were systematically tortured and put to death in large numbers. The memory of this horror has been shrouded, as traumatic memories are, but it is as unresolved as all the rest of our traumatic legacy.

Contrary to the mythologies of the perpetrators, trauma always leaves its mark. The heritage of slavery is a central unacknowledged wound in U.S. society that haunts the descendants of slave and slave holder alike. The massive thefts and attempted genocide inflicted on Native American peoples lie just under the surface of daily life, in the pretense that there are no living heirs to those cultures, in the obsessive way we name everything from cars to pencils to blue jeans after indigenous nations, in the way as a culture we hunger for souvenirs of what our ancestors tried to destroy.

The trauma of the witch persecutions has been deeply buried under myths of enlightenment and celebrations of conquest, rationalized as a scientific crusade against superstition or, at worst, shrugged off as a minor error of our collective youth. There are no monuments, official apologies, days of collective mourning. We have not had the opportunity to reconstruct the story. We have not had the collective will to pull back the veil. Perhaps it will be those women who are survivors of privatized sexual tortures who will best be able to bear witness to the long nightmare of state-sanctioned ritual abuse and show us the strands of the web that bind us to those events.

One of the common accusations against witches is nightflying: the ability to change shape or endow a household object, a pot or broom, with magical powers and soar above the landscape of daily life, with eyes that can penetrate the darkness and see what we are not supposed to see. From these forbidden heights one can see the lines of extinct roads and old riverbeds, the designs made by private land holdings, the relationships between water and growth, the proximity or distances between people. Those who can see in the dark can uncover secrets: hidden comings and goings, deals and escapes, the undercover movements of troops, layers of life normally conducted out of sight.

Nightflying requires a willingness to leave the familiar ground and see what is meant to be hidden, a willingness to be transformed. If we are to know and understand the landscape of our history, we must be willing to do this: not only to look upon the horrific, the night shadowed, and bear witness to it, but to see its place in the whole, to see that the road to the square where a dozen women and girls are burning to death is the ordinary market road, winding between the houses of people whose faces we mostly know, and that the wood that stokes the flames was neatly stacked behind their houses all along.

The Politics of Childhood

Childhood is the one political condition, the one disenfranchised group through which all people pass. The one constituency of the oppressed in which all surviving members eventually stop being members and have the option of becoming administrators of the same conditions for new members.

All adults share the privileges of adulthood and the memories of systematic subjugation, humiliation and control—even those who were not treated with cruelty as children, who had loving parents with good parenting skills, still experienced arbitrary decisions, disrespect, patronization, ridicule, control over our eating, involuntary confinement.

The oppression of children is the wheel that keeps all other oppressions turning. Without it, misery would have to be imposed afresh on each new generation, instead of being passed down like a heritage of disease. Children enter the world full of expectation and hope. They are not jaded. They are not cynical or resigned. They see clearly what custom has made invisible to us, and are outraged by all injustices, no matter how small. It is through the agency of former children that the revolutionary potential of each generation of children is held in check.

This does not need to be deliberate or malicious. The disempowerment we all experienced as children has little outlet. We are taught to obey until our own turn comes, with few opportunities to politicize the experience and critique it. Instead we spend billions of dollars in therapy, attempting to unraveling it at a personal level. We have deeply internalized the appropriateness of childhood's rules and regulations. Because the condition is not permanent and the nature of it changes throughout our childhood years, it is difficult to develop a collective political response to the injustices. At the same time, because it is not permanent, because we pass through it and know we will, some of us are able to make and keep commitments to remember what we know about childhood and make it different for the next generation.

Childhood has never been, except for relatively small numbers of the class privileged, a protected time of sweetness. Children make up the majority of the world's poorest people. Children are the most vulnerable to sexual abuse and exploitation. The working conditions of child labor worldwide are so bad that they are often indistinguishable from slavery. Without any form of political representation, children remain in many senses the property of the adults in their lives. It is illegal for them to run away. The fact that many parents are deeply loving, fair and committed to their children's well-being does not change the fact that this is largely a matter of luck for the child, that she or he has almost no control over the conditions of daily life.

We tolerate and accept for children a level of disenfranchisement that we would protest for any other constituency. Childhood is the standard for acceptable powerlessness. "They're just like children" is the classic statement of paternalistic racism and patriarchy. "Don't treat me like a child" is the outraged cry of the disrespected. We talk about the ways in which various groups are not admitted to full adulthood, how women were and in many places still are permanent legal minors, how the colonized are considered naive, not ready for self-governance, deprived of sovereignty with the same air of protectiveness we extend to the young.

In fact, the arguments against the enfranchisement of children are identical to those used to oppose suffrage for women, immigrants, former slaves, the illiterate and the poor in general. "They are innocent and cannot understand politics. They will be taken advantage of and manipulated by the political interests of those more sophisticated than they. They aren't ready for the responsibility." But what readies people for responsibility is being allowed to take some. People become informed and savvy about those areas of life where they can exercise some power. It is powerlessness that creates passivity. When children are treated with respect, given choice and expected to have opinions that matter, they have opinions and make choices. I wonder what it must have been like, what dignity it must have conferred on children of the Iroquois Confederacy that any child over three was welcome to speak about matters of group importance in the tribal councils.

One of the most politicizing experiences of my life was the summer I spent in Cuba when I was fourteen. I found myself in a country in which fourteen-year-olds could make life decisions for themselves—to join the merchant marine, drill in the militia, choose special training—

without parental permission. Suddenly adults were asking me what I thought the Johnson administration was going to do about this or that aspect of the war, where the U.S. economy was headed, what the long-term impact of the Black Panthers would be... But the real shock was returning to Chicago at the end of the summer. Once again I had to sit in enforced boredom in homeroom, raise my hand to go to the bathroom, get written permission to be in the hallway and get picked up by the police for being outdoors after 10 p.m. or as a suspected runaway for being anywhere they didn't think a teenage girl should be. And my circumstances were very mild compared to those of many young people I knew.

Nevertheless, children resist, both their own condition and the pressures to take on the perpetrator roles of the adults around them. Children have far less tolerance for overt injustice than do adults. From Soweto to Managua we have seen young people take to the streets and force the issue, propelling mass movements forward into open rebellion almost faster than adults could build organizations behind them.

It is exciting and hopeful to me not only that are we seeing a growing international movement around child labor issues, but that children are taking strong leadership in it. Pakistani carpet weaver Iqbal Massih escaped from employers who had held him in virtual slavery from early childhood and immediately began speaking and organizing other child laborers. He had decided he wanted to become a lawyer when he grew up, in order to continue this work. He traveled to many countries meeting with young students and building support for child labor campaigns. Then one day while riding his bike he was gunned down. High-school students in Massachusetts who had met with him got on the Internet and raised hundreds of thousands of dollars to establish a school in his name for child workers in Pakistan. Canadian Craig Keilberger, moved by this story, also became in international organizer and public speaker, forcing the Canadian government to include child labor issues in trade negotiations with Pakistan.

Children's liberation is being spearheaded by street children and child laborers in Latin America, Asia and Africa and by the poorest inhabitants of the rich nations. Just as white abolitionists had to struggle with the desire to patronize and control the efforts of ex-slaves, as adults we need to back the initiatives of children themselves, helping them secure resources and offering expertise, but respecting their right and ability to lead themselves and learning to let them lead us. In doing so we will bring powerful new resources to a wide range of struggles. We will be able to bring into our own awareness, and begin to repair, the places where childhood disempowered us. And we will begin dismantling one of the most powerful mechanisms through which oppression reproduces itself.

~Speaking in Tongues

On Not Writing English

About five years ago I was dickering with an editor, a feminist academic, about the changes she wanted to make in an article of mine, when she informed me that a line I had written was not English. She didn't mean that it was in Spanish or Swahili and would I please translate. She meant that the way I danced through syntax made her uneasy, that the grammar wasn't stacking up the way she liked it. She was reminding me that she had a certificate of legitimacy and I didn't. "Sure it's English," I replied. "It's just not your English." "No, really," she insisted. "It's not good English."

Good English, as I understand it, is a set of agreements about which words make sense, what they mean and in what order they need to be used in order to keep making sense. It's an attempt to make sure that we understand each other. This is a reasonable goal. But the group that makes up these agreements and sets them down in rule books is a tiny fraction of the multitudes of people who successfully communicate in the English language each and every day.

What's more, these legislators of language, like those of government, are almost exclusively male, white and wealthy, unlike the majority of English speakers. They are people with social power, and as is the wont of such folk, they set things up according to their own very specific needs and then declare those needs universal: if it isn't the language we speak, it isn't English.

I ain't gonna say ain't no more, 'cause ain't *ain't in the dictionary*. But some of the best English ain't. I am the daughter of a Bronx Puerto Rican mother and a Brooklyn Ashkenazi Jewish father, both college educated, both in love with literature. I grew up reading 19th- and 20th-century English novels, short stories and poetry from England and the United States, most of it by white women and men of privilege. I speak that language and enjoy reading it. But there are some days when only the savory smokiness of a Southern-Black-English-come-north-to-Chicago or the fancy code-switchin' salsera footwork of New York street Spanglish will do. They are no more or less mine by birth than the rolling English prose of George Eliot or the sharply stitched phrases of Jane Austen, but who in their right senses could deny the juiciness, the aliveness, the *rightness* of such rich talk?

I am also the child of a bilingual family that delights in tongue acrobatics of mixed syntax and vocabulary. We write as we speak, in run-on sentences (if Faulkner could do it and be called great, why can't we?); in sentence fragments (if it's broken up on the page, it's called poetry); in a Spanglish that freely combines the best of several worlds (like Saxons and Normans sitting down together to eat: pass the maldito venison, I mean the haunch of deer). What we create eventually passes into the dictionaries, because it is we who create language, the working people who are the majority. We refuse to use some talks and insist on others, and slowly, with plenty of squeaking, the gates open a crack and another "colloquialism" slips through. The process of "corruption," of making "bad English," is the same process that creates any language. A slow volcanic seepage from below, constantly lifting up new mountains ranges; shifting earth, a sudden avalanche, people moving, adapting, finding new ways to say things and new things to say. Just as the Normans brought "poultry" to squat alongside "fowl," the English put on pyjamas in India, and Puerto Rican men in the U.S. army turned "safety can" into *zafacón* and took it home to fill up with banana peels.

Don't get me wrong. I appreciate grammar. It's as useful as a good hoe for breaking up clods—those muddy clumps of language in which we find the woman sitting on the chair with green eyes and other oddities. But a hoe is a tool, not a gardener. A hoe can't tell you whether to plant sweet peas or okra. That depends on whether you have a greater need for color and scent, or big pot of gumbo.

Just last month it happened again. Asked to write from my very Puerto Rican Jewish poet perspective on a thorny little piece of island politics, yet another white academic feminist editor slashed her way through my prose, cutting out the personal pronouns through which I proclaimed my presence in the debates and pumping it full of Latinate words. I told her I was not generic. That when I said "our" about my own culture, it was not a question of grammar, but of politics; that when she crossed it out she was refusing to acknowledge that my "our" was different from hers, which in fact was the reason I was asked to write that particular essay, and that to seek out the insights of women of color and attempt to repackage them in someone else's language is opportunistic and disrespectful.

This is not a new conversation. Years ago, when I was a student at Mills College, a professor there told me that the problem with my stories was that they didn't spend enough time inside the individual angst of a central character and were much too concerned with community, and by the way, I should eliminate my sprinkling of Spanish words, since there was no audience for bilingual literature. It had never occurred to her that I wrote about community on purpose, within a strong Latin American tradition of collective protagonists, that I wasn't writing the way I did from a lack of technical skill.

It's a Catch-22 kind of deal. Rejecting the centrality of the elites is proof of our inferior understanding. Those who make up the rules of Good English try earnestly or contemptuously to edit us into conformity, convinced that when we talk a different talk it's because we are educationally or genetically impaired.

The fact is, as a steady diet, we find cucumber sandwiches, lamb stew, even crusty French bread tedious. Human speech is filled with delicious regional cuisines, spicy as Cajun peppers, delicate as almond curd. You mix basil with lemon grass, garlic with ginger, achiote with oregano: new dishes evolve every day as we trade flavors and ingredients from continents brought ever closer by the international marketplace.

It's not that we can't do baguettes and brie. All peoples under attack learn the languages of those who can do us harm. We are multilingual of necessity. Those of us who, by using that language successfully, gain access to a small piece of public ground must fight continually to push our authenticity into print, onto the airwaves, into the classroom, out from the podium. We walk the narrow line of strategy, wielding Good English like a club against the self-absorbed arrogance of those who want to hear only themselves speak, clearing spaces where we can broadcast our home voices, the kitchen talk and backyard talk, street and front-porch talk that will choke us if we swallow it for too long. It's a guerrilla war against linguistic control where sassy slangs and precision-calibrated formalities are wielded in turn, as needed.

A day will come when our linguistic versatility will be excavated and displayed as a national treasure, when "English only" and "Good English only" will be ancient barbarities of self-defeating closed-mindedness, studied in astonishment by schoolchildren who are as proud of the distinctive and varied flavors of talk they command as the most popular chefs in a contest of international and regional cookery.

In the meantime, remember that little red pencil may get you convicted of war crimes against the creativity of our children. Remember that if you refuse our speech, you'll be left out of the conversation. Our numbers are growing, our languages multiplying and opening up the pavement like tough-rooted mint, like fists of crabgrass, like wildflowers in bloom.

Forked Tongues

On Not Speaking Spanish[1]

~ *1* ~

To understand what we prose writers of the diaspora are doing, it is necessary to know why and how we are writing. Storytelling is a basic human activity with which we simultaneously make and understand the world and our place in it.

The world in which U.S. Puerto Rican writing takes place, the context that most profoundly determines its form, is racism. Racism firmly rooted in class, in both the original class identities of those who migrated and in the enforcement of a persistent poverty on the diaspora community. Unrelenting racism that permeates our daily lives in all its forms, from brutality and humiliation at the hands of the police, schools and other institutions to the most subtle ways of making us disappear as human beings. Our history is stolen from us. We are stripped of our names. We are made into caricatures in a burlesque written by those who despise us or know nothing at all of us.

So the first and most important thing to understand is that we write from necessity; that our writing is a form of cultural and spiritual self-defense. To live surrounded by a popular culture in which we do not appear is a form of spiritual erasure that leaves us vulnerable to all the assaults a society can commit against those it does not recognize. Not to be recognized, not to find oneself in history, or in film, or on television, or in books, or in popular songs, or in what is studied at school leads to the psychic disaster of ceasing to recognize oneself. Our literature is documentation of an existence that doesn't matter a damn to those in charge. And like the forged passports of my paternal Jewish relatives, from time to time it saves our lives.

This is why we write: to see ourselves on the page. To confirm our presence. To clear a space where we can examine the lives we live, not as the sexy girlfriends, petty crooks and crime victims of TV cop shows, and not as statistical profiles in which hardship, bravery and resource-fulness lose all personality, but in our own physical and emotional reality. Where we can pull apart and explore this complex relationship we have with the island of our origins and kinship, and this vast many-peopled country in which we are writing a new chapter of Puerto Ricanhood. This necessity gives shape to our literature, to our urgent poetry of the streets, our ever-so-autobiographical fiction, our legends of collective identity. Most of what we write, we write under pressure.

~2~

And we do it in English, in Spanish, in a delicious blend of the two. Because one of our most important tools has been our creativity with language. Our linguistic sabotage, right and left. Anglo-American words transformed into Puerto Ricanisms revealing no trace of their gringo ancestry, like zafacón, the seedless oranges renamed nebos and the Irish name O'Hara made into a generic code for the New York City police, la jara.

Words we borrow from Jewish neighbors, African-American cowork-ers, Irish-American nuns. We have invented the language we most needed, and it is at least as authentic as the well-educated Spanish, with its baroque flourishes, of any scholarly poet with a university sponsor-ship.

Like any language, it is born from history. The Spanish, or rather Spanishes, that are used on the island grew out of an identical process of change and accumulation: Taíno fragments sticking to places and plants, Africanisms of daily use, traces of the Berber conquest of Spain like the countrywoman's hopeful "ojalá," may it come to pass, O Allah. Particular juicy tidbits from dozens of passionately particular places in Spain; idiomatic baggage brought by refugees fleeing American revolu-tions from Haiti to Colombia; linguistic recipes and verbal cuttings carried by Corsican, Mallorcan, French, Caribbean and U.S. immigrants of the last century. Adding the professional and popular anglicisms of this century is just salt in the sancocho.

~3~

Because our writing is testimony, written under pressure, in words we invent to describe what official language is totally inadequate for, we specialize in fiction with an autobiographical flavor. In the cultural context of racism, sometimes autobiography approaches science fiction or what incredulous outsiders persist in seeing as magical realism. But so far, tales of invention and the fantastic have not interested us as much as the defiance of our daily lives. It is there that we struggle for an authentic cultural terrain, in which we are what we are, without asking anyone's pardon. Only in this way can we go beyond nostalgia on the one hand and camouflage on the other. In our multi-genre collection, *Getting Home Alive,* my mother, Rosario Morales, writes: "I am what I am... Boricua as Boricuas come from the isle of Manhattan...Take it or leave me alone." And I respond: "I am a child of the Americas... I am new, history made me. My first language was Spanglish. I was born at the crossroads, and I am whole."

~4~

And what of our relationship to literary and cultural production on the island? The greatest obstacle, until very recently, to the development of this relationship has been arrogance. Arrogance of class, race and gender with a strong flavor of the nationalistic and the patriarchal. That same arrogance that the migrants, always the poorest and darkest of our population, always those women who, for lack of resources or inclination, couldn't play their assigned role in the stories of the señores, hoped to leave behind them. This disdain for the oppressed, one of those inherited luxuries the regime continues to permit to the colonial elite, has framed all attempts at dialogue. The island elite persists in seeing the creators of this new diaspora culture as runaway children who lack the maturity and discrimination to return to the Hispanic house from which we supposedly came, although the African house has housed us through generations of exile and rebellion, and we have lived in a house of American mestizaje for a very long time now.

Those who partake of this anachronistic view tend to see our writings as scribbles in the margins of real literature, undeserving of serious study. They market their books to Argentina and Mexico and turn their cultured backs with a shudder on Hartford and Philadelphia. The Real Academia, supremely irrelevant as it is to the South Bronx, continues to be at the least a point of navigation to those who feel that three generations of creative ferment in Harlem have nothing to say to them.

The truth is that nearly half of all Puerto Ricans have taken part in the creation of this new culture, and it is more than possible that the future vitality of island culture will depend on recognizing and celebrating this fact.

~5~

Migration has changed us in more than geographical ways. In spite of our passionate identification with the island and its people, we are no longer who we were. Ours is a diaspora continually in motion, swinging between the island of Puerto Rico and the cities of the United States.[2] To the degree that the realities of this continually shifting life have freed us of the nostalgic idealizations of earlier generations, it has become possible for us to look at island society with new eyes.

The same constant negotiations of identity that come with a multi-lingual, multicultural, multi-landscape existence give us a sharp ear for unspoken social arrangements that perhaps requires distance and dis-possession. We are part of one extended family, but we live under a different roof, and from here, we have a new angle on the family scandals, among them a racism that is less segregated, but no less deep-rooted and wounding, than that of the United States.

A personal example. During my childhood in Puerto Rico, my father worked as an associate professor on a modest salary. But in Indiera Baja of Maricao, where I grew up, having any kind of a salary made you rich. In a community where many women still cooked outdoors over a wood fire, hauled water from a spring, washed all clothing by hand, where the first refrigerators had barely arrived and where cash hardly ever passed through women's hands, to be the daughter of a professor was to be privileged almost to the point of aristocracy. What's more, I was one of the blanquitas. They called me rubia and americanita. Perhaps if my family had stayed there, I would have accepted, with a greater or lesser degree of comfort, this role of artificial importance.

But at the age of thirteen I was taken to Chicago, and was suddenly transformed from the American's daughter, to the daughter of that Puerto Rican from Harlem who laughs too much and talks with her hands. From almost aristocracy, to a lesser level of the academic middle class, and most of all, from rubia to spic. At the same time that I lost my literal color in the long winters of Illinois, I acquired social color. In my new world, I was defined by others, and eventually by myself, as a U.S. woman of color. In this broad community born of collective resistance to our grinding down by gender and so-called race, in the vital conversations among American women who were African, Chinese, Japanese,

Chicana, I was apprenticed. I was born as a writer within a literary movement that is anti-racist, feminist and very, very multicultural, where among so much struggle for our full legitimacy, being an immigrant Puerto Rican Jew didn't cause anyone to bat an eye.

~6~

In my case, this was the most important transformation: the detailed and sophisticated understanding of how day-to-day racism acts, what it smells like, what face it wears. It's a kind of sixth sense acquired by those who need it. For my mother, the essential thing was her identification with working people from every continent, whom the currents of the world market had deposited in the neighborhoods of New York. For Carmen de Monteflores, it was the physical and cultural distance that allowed her, in her novel *Cantando Bajito/Singing Softly*, to examine the consequences of class, race and illicit sexual encounters in three generations of an island family something like her own. Judith Ortiz Cofer, in her autobiography in prose and poetry, *Silent Dancing*, uses the double vision of her nomadic life between Puerto Rico and New Jersey to explore the dangers and delights, bitterness and confusion of female sexuality in Puerto Rican culture.

Yes, another thing that can be seen from under this other roof is the rigidity of the island patriarch. In a small and gossip-ridden island, anything you do anywhere is known to everyone, making it much easier for him to enforce the social controls of his regime. In the gigantic, anonymous cities where most of the migrants have landed there are traditions already many generations old of defiance of social norms. City people are used to nonconformity, and it's easy to live all kinds of lives, the rumors of which will never reach your parents' living room. This liberalism of urban life persists, even in a period of social repression such as we have experienced in recent years, and it provides vital support for the development of a wider range of gender identities and sexual behaviors among immigrant Puerto Ricans, women and men.[3]

The literature of the diaspora is a literature of multiple vision, born of the intersections of oppression and resistance. This multiplicity has given us the tools to challenge inherited identities of gender, class and "race," and through it we have found a way to affirm our complex realities. It is this complexity, this many-sided seeing, this daring to name the uses and practices of power wherever they are found, that is our greatest gift—to the emerging cultures of the diaspora and to the changing island culture of Puerto Rico.

Notes

1. This essay was originally given as a talk at the University of Mayaquez in April 1992, as part of a conference of island and diaspora writers, celebrating Semana de la Lengua, or Spanish language week. Since that time there have been major improvements in relations between writers and intellectuals in the two communities, including many new collaborations.

2. This is not the case of the Hawaiian Puerto Rican community, much of which has had no contact with the island since the turn of the century.

3. The degree to which homophobia in Puerto Rico represents a significant factor in migration has yet to be explored. Anecdotally though, many young Puerto Ricans in the United States have told me that this was major reason for their own departure.

Certified Organic Intellectual
On Not Being Postmodern

I have begun this essay a hundred times, in a hundred different ways, and each time I have struggled with the same deadly numbing of my mind. Hashing it out once again with my parents on the phone, this time we go for the food metaphors. When I was a child in rural Puerto Rico, the people around me ate produce grown on local soil, chickens that roamed the neighborhood, bananas cut from the stalk. It was unrefined, unpackaged, full of all those complex nutrients that get left out when the process is too tightly controlled. But during the last few years before we emigrated, advertising finally penetrated into our remote part of the island. Cheez Whiz on Wonder Bread was sold to country women as a better, more sophisticated, modern, advanced and healthy breakfast than boiled root vegetables and codfish or rice and beans.

When I call myself an organic intellectual, I mean that the ideas I carry with me were grown on soil I know, that I can tell you about the mineral balance, the weather, the labor involved in preparing them for use. In the marketplace of ideas, we are pushed toward the supermarket chains that are replacing the tiny rural colmado; told that store-bought is better, imported is best; and sold on empty calories in shiny packaging instead of open crates and barrels of produce to which the earth still clings.

The intellectual traditions I come from create theory out of shared lives instead of sending away for it. My thinking grew directly out of listening to my own discomforts, finding out who shared them, who validated them, and in exchanging stories about common experiences, finding patterns, systems, explanations of how and why things happened. This is the central process of consciousness raising, of collective testimonio. This is how homemade theory happens.

In the women's consciousness-raising groups I belonged to in the early 1970s, we shared personal and very emotional stories of what it had really been like for us to live as women, examining our experiences with men and with other women in our families, sexual relationships, workplaces and schools, in the health care system and in surviving the general societal contempt and violence toward women. As we told our stories we found validation that our experiences and our reactions to them were common to many women, that our perceptions, thoughts and feelings made sense to other women. We then used that shared experience as a source of authority. Where our lives did not match official knowledge we trusted our lives, and used the collective and mutually validated body of stories to critique those official versions of reality. This was theory born of an activist need, and the feminist literature we read, from articles like "The Politics of Housework" and "The Myth of the Vaginal Orgasm" to the poetry of Susan Griffin, Marge Piercy and Alta, rose out of the same mass phenomenon of truth-telling from personal knowledge.

I am also the child of two cultures of resistance. I grew up jíbara, a word that means countrified and is used both to romanticize the imaginary simple and noble coffee workers of yesteryear and as a put-down somewhat akin to hick. But it originally meant, in the language of the Arawak people, "she who runs away to be free," referring to the mixed-blood settlements of escaped slaves, fugitive Indians and European peasants who took to the mountains to escape state control. I was raised in one of those settlements, listening to women talk.

I also grew up in a family of activists who were thinking about race and class and gender and the uses of history and literature long before there were college courses to do this in, a mother who was a feminist in the 1950s, a father who told me bedtime stories about African and Chinese history and taught biology as a liberation science. I grew up as the tropical branch of a tribe of working-class Jewish thinkers who were critiquing the canons of their day from the shtetls of Eastern Europe, arguing about identity politics and coalitions, assimilation and solidarity way back into the last century. How I think and what I think about grows from my identity as a jíbara shtetl intellectual and organizer. I was taught to trust in these traditions, in the reliability of my own intelligence combined with that of others.

But as academic feminism drifts farther and farther from its activist roots, as the elite gobbledygook of postmodernist jargon makes it less and less acceptable to speak comprehensibly, I have more and more often found my trust in myself under assault.

I watch my life and my theorizing about it become the raw materials of someone else's expertise, and I am reminded of the neem tree of India, used for millennia as an insect repellent, now being patented by a multinational pharmaceutical company. Peasant women developed the technology for extracting and preparing the oil for local use, but to multinationals, local use is a waste. The exact same process, done at much higher volume, and packaged for export, is what they have been able to patent. My intellectual life and that of other organic intellectuals, many of them women of color, is fully sophisticated enough for use. But in order to have value in the marketplace, the entrepreneurs and multinational developers must find a way to process it, to refine the rich multiplicity of our lives and all we have come to understand about them into high theory by the simple act of removing it, abstracting it beyond recognition, taking out the fiber, boiling it down until the vitality is oxidized away and then marketing it as their own and selling it back to us for more than we can afford.

*****

The local colmado of Barrio Rubias, which is just across the road from Barrio Indiera Baja where I was raised, used to sell two kinds of cheese. Queso holandés, Dutch cheese, came in great big balls covered with red wax. If it molded, it did so from the outside in, so the center remained good, and one could trim the green from the rind. Or you could buy something called "imitation processed cheese food product." Both began in the mammary glands of cows. But the processed "cheese food product," like its modern relatives Velveeta or the individually plastic-wrapped Kraft singles, was barely identifiable with any of the processes of its production, and what's more, when it spoiled, it did so thoroughly. All the capacity for resistance of a solid cheese with a rind had been refined away. Nevertheless, the processed cheese often sold better. The packaging was colorful, mysteriously sealed, difficult to open.

We have been well trained to be consumers of glossy boxes, Ziploc bags, childproof bottles and copious amounts of plastic wrap and cellophane. We are taught to be distrustful of bulk foods and to rely on brand-name recognition. The students I work with have been taught to give books so much more authority than they give their own lives that, with the best will to comply, they find it very challenging to write autobiographical responses to the readings and lectures. What they know best how to do is arrange the published opinions of other people in a logical sequence, restating one or another school of thought on the topic at hand.

When the package is difficult to penetrate, they rarely ask why the damn thing has to be wrapped up so tight. They assume the problem is with them. When I first re-entered higher education, as a middle-aged professional writer with many years of public speaking behind me, even with all the confidence these things gave me, I felt humiliated by the impenetrable language in which academic thinking comes wrapped these days. But I thought it was just a matter of overcoming my awkwardness with jargon. A problem of lack of training. Like recently decolonized countries that embrace all the shiny wonders of nuclear energy, determined to have what the empire has had all along, I thought this slick new arrangement of words just needed to be acquired.

But I no longer think this. The language in which ideas are expressed is never neutral. The language people use reveals important information about who they identify with, what their intentions are, for whom they are writing or speaking. The packaging is the product being sold, and does exactly what is was designed for. Unnecessarily specialized language is used to humiliate those who are not supposed to feel entitled. It sells the illusion that only those who can wield it can think.

A frequent response to those who resist exclusive language is that they are intellectually lazy. As with other forms of gatekeeping, the gate is treated as a natural feature of the landscape, and overcoming it as a rite of passage perfectly designed to measure our worth. If it slows us down, it just means we weren't supposed to get in. If in spite of this we decide we want entry anyway, we must stop what we are doing, forget what we came for and devote our energies to techniques of breaking and entering (no-one suggests blowing the damn thing off its hinges). We are required to do this just to win the right to argue. If we are uninterested, we are assumed to be incompetent. But my choice to read the readable has to do with a different set of priorities. Language is wedded to content, and the content I seek is theory and intellectual practice that will be of use to me in an activist scholarship whose priorities are democratizing.

*****

At the time that I was first struggling to hold onto my own intellectual integrity within academia I had little validation in my daily life for these feelings. I struggled to be "good" and do as I was supposed to, felt that I must be missing something when most of what I read seemed shallow or irrelevant to my work, felt that somehow feminist theory should be more exciting to me, that maybe it was a lack of academic skill that was the problem. But most of what I read seemed so many levels of abstraction away from activist intentions and lived experience, from the problems I wanted to solve, that it had become an intellectual exercise, academic in that other sense of the word—disconnected from daily use. To fully understand it, to really engage and argue in that place, I would have had to abandon what I cared most about and devote major energy to the study of a history of ideas instead of doing my chosen work with and about my own peoples.

Now, looking back, I remember my life in the feminist movement of the early 1980s. At conference after conference I would stand in the hall trying to choose between the workshop or caucus for women of color and the one for Jews. How every doorway I tried to enter required leaving some part of myself behind. In those hallways I began meeting other women, the complexity of whose lives defied the simplifications of identity politics. In conversation with them I found the only reflections of my full reality. Much of the feminist theory I tried to read during graduate school was written in rooms whose doors were too narrow. They required me to leave myself and my deepest intellectual passions outside.

The place of validation I finally found was with those same women, the ones who had survived against all odds, in this case Latina feminist scholars who, the moment we found a venue to gather and talk alone, began making theory out of the stuff in our pockets, out of the stories, incidents, dreams, frustrations that were never acceptable anywhere else.

Now I know that the complexity of unrefined food is far more nourishing than the processed stuff. I know that theorizing, placing ourselves in context, grounding ourselves in the work of others_happens much more effectively at the farmers' market than at Safeway, hapens best where the work that brought it to the table is most visible.

I return to one of the first poems I wrote:

Poetry
is something refined
in your vocabulary
taking its place at the table
in a silver bowl.
I come from the earth
where the cane was grown…
My poems grow from the ground.

~Raíces

Raícism

Rootedness as Spiritual and Political Practice

~*1*~

Raícism—from raíces or roots—is the practice of rooting ourselves in the real, concrete histories of our people: our families, our local communities, our ethnic communities. It is radical genealogy, history made personal. It is a keeping of accounts. Its intent is to pierce the immense, mind-deadening denial that permeates daily life the United States, that drowns our deepest grief and horror about the founding and ongoing atrocities of racism, class and patriarchy in an endless chatter about trivialities. Oppression buries the actual lives of real and contradictory people in the crude generalizations of bigotry and punishes us for not matching the caricature, refusing all evidence of who we actually are in defiance of its tidy categories. It is a blunt instrument, used for bashing, not only our dangerous complexities, but also the ancient and permanent fact of our involvement with each other.

Raícism, or rootedness, is the choice to bear witness to our specific, contradictory, historical identities in relationship to one another. The decision to examine exactly who our ancestors, all of them, have been—with each other and with everyone else. It is an accounting of the debts and assets we have inherited, and acknowledging the precise nature of that inheritance is an act of spiritual and political integrity.

~*2*~

I grew up on stories of my mother's barrio childhood in Spanish Harlem and the Bronx, of near starvation in the early years of the

Depression, of my grandmother's single dress. It was not until I went to the small Puerto Rican town of Toa Alta and examined the parish registers that I discovered five generations of slave-holding ancestors among the petty landed gentry of northeast Puerto Rico. For generations a handful of families held political and economic power, married their children to each other and consolidated their wealth with the purchase of enslaved human beings. I remember the feelings, as this reality dawned on me, of shame, but also of excitement. Over the years I had found peasants, small farmers, revolutionaries in my family tree. This was the thing I had not wanted to find. If I could figure out how to face it and consciously carry it, how to transform shame and denial into wholeness, perhaps I could find a way out of the numbness of privilege, not only for myself, but for the people I worked with in classes and workshops who came asking to learn.

So that day I wrote down the name of each and every slave held by my ancestors that I could find recorded in the registers. I have used my own family history with slavery to break silence: to acknowledge publicly and repeatedly my family debt to their coerced labor, to expose and reject family mythology about our "kind" treatment of slaves as a step in challenging the generalized myth of kind slavery in Puerto Rico, and to make a decision that although none of these people had chosen me as a descendant, I owed them the respect one gives to ancestors because their labor had made it possible for my forebears to grow up and thrive. I have also made it my responsibility to make African people visible in every discussion of Puerto Rican history in which I participate.

Taking full responsibility for the legacy of relationships that our ancestors have left us is empowering and radical. Guilt and denial and the urgently defensive pull to avoid blame require immense amounts of energy and are profoundly immobilizing. Giving them up can be a great relief. Deciding that we are in fact accountable frees us to act. Acknowledging our ancestors' participation in the oppression of others (and this is ultimately true of everyone if you really dig) and deciding to balance the accounts on their behalf leads to greater integrity and less shame, less self-righteousness and more righteousness, humility and compassion and a sense of proportion.

At the same time, uncovering the credit side of the accounts, not the suffering but the solidarity, persistence, love, hard work, creativity and soul of our forebears is also an obligation we owe them. We are the ones responsible for carrying that forward into our own time and for calling on our kin to do likewise. For people committed to liberation to claim our descent from the perpetrators is a renewal of faith in human beings.

If slavers, invaders, committers of genocide, inquisitors can beget abolitionists, resistance fighters, healers, community builders, then anyone
can transform an inheritance of privilege or of victimization into something more fertile than either.

One of the rewards of discovering exactly who our people have
been—and how and with whom they have lived—is the possibility of
unimagined kinship. My Jewish ancestors were settled in the Ukraine as
a buffer against Turkish invasion, alongside German Mennonites
brought in to teach the formerly landless Jews about farming. At a talk
in Wichita, Kansas, I was able to thank their descendants and claim a
relationship between us, as Eastern European Jew and German Christian, other than that of genocidal anti-Semitism.

Mapping the specificity of our ethnicity also reveals hidden relationships. European Americans in this country need to find out in relationship to whom they became white. The answers will be very different for
the descendants of a Scot from Iowa, an Irishwoman from Alabama, a
New York Pole, a Louisiana French-Spanish Creole, a Texan with roots
in 17th-century England and 19th-century Austria and a Romanian Jew
who settled in turn-of-the-century San Francisco. Questions about our
place within the megastructures of racism become intimate and carry
personality. It becomes possible to see the choices we make right now as
extensions of those inherited ones, and to choose more courageously as
a result.

What Race Isn't

Teaching Racism

The biggest challenge in teaching about racism is to hold double vision. On the one hand, tc continually point out that the seemingly real, obvious and biological foundations of racial categories are completely fabricated, constantly shifting and, in spite of their widespread acceptance, not obvious at all. On the other, to explicitly map, over and over again, the devastating injuries brought about by racism, and expose the ways that ideas of race are used to justify gross economic and social inequities.

It's a tightrope walk requiring dexterity in handling contradiction. To expose the notion of biological race as fraudulent, to look at the actual genetics of human diversity and see that there is no such thing as race, no human subspecies, without allowing any quarter to the liberal pretensions of color blindness, to the literal whitewashing of real differences in culture, experience, power, resources. To demolish the idea of fundamental biological difference and refuse to let anyone get away with "we're all human beings," meaning "we're all like me."

To bear witness to the bloody history of racism, to expose the manipulations and brutalities, the wicked roots of the ideologies and their ruthless implementation, and to make ample space for righteous rage without allowing a speck of essentialism to creep into the anger of students of color, conceding no space at all to ideas of "blood" determining our moral and political stances.

It is extremely useful to teach students about the flexibility of racial notions, how adaptable they are to the needs of the elite. To see the usefulness of racism to those who wield it. What does it mean that early in this century, Finnish immigrants, pale as they were, and in spite of all the expert testimony of the race experts of the day, were ruled in a court of law to be non-white, based on "common sense"? Or that mid-19th-century debates in California classified the Chinese as Black and the Mexicans as white, not because of their features but because of their relative positions in the economy of the time and place? And to see how 150 years have reversed that classification: Mexican Americans are most definitely no longer seen as white, while Asian Americans, economically exploited as the immigrant population continues to be, are considered the people of color closest to "almost white," and that this has more to do with the economic rise of Japan and the industrialization of parts of the Pacific Rim than with any increased tolerance or enlightenment among European Americans.[1]

It's in that space of critical curiosity and historical context, in the tension held between layers of truth, that insight emerges. Those moments of insight in my own life came from being abruptly shifted across categories in the eyes of others. In 1967 my family moved from rural Puerto Rico to Chicago. On the island my light brown hair was called "rubia" or blonde, and although I was a Latin American girl and a colonial subject, my middle-class access in a community of farm laborers, my U.S. Jewish father and my light skin color made me a "blanquita."

In Chicago, in the private university high school my father's faculty status entitled us to, my brother and I became *spics* overnight. My skin color became lighter in the long sunless winters and my English was accent-free, something that people still marvel over in congratulatory voices. But as a Puerto Rican girl in a big U.S. city, I acquired social color. Some of us are dark enough and Spanish-speaking enough to bear the brunt of immediate and constant recognition and unambiguous classification as a target. Others, like me, become the tokens, exotic but acceptable. We are the ones who are told we don't look Puerto Rican, don't sound Puerto Rican, the ones who are always being invited to collude in despising our kinfolk, the ones people confide their racism to as between friends.

Redefined by others as a young woman of color, and fortunate enough to find communities of activism where I could give voice to the complexity of my social identities, feminist women of color became my home and the root place of my political coming of age. But "woman of color" is essentially a political definition, not a racial one. It is a name that does not belong to every female with dark skin and ancestors from outside of Europe. It's a name defined by collective opposition to racism, a unity defined by a politicized shared experience. It brings together peoples who have been at war with one another for centuries. It brings together people whose features, colors, languages, customs have very little in common, but who, confronted with U.S. racism, were redefined in similar ways, subjected to similar abuses.

Just as "white" was invented to cover all those invited to partake of colonial pie, some sooner, some later, and defined always, against someone else's not-whiteness. In 1744, when sailors pressed into the service of England joined with indentured servants, slaves, relocated indigenous people and others to riot against the elite of New York City and burn their mansions, English sailors spoke of going out to attack white people as if it were obvious that this category did not include them. European immigrants came to this country Irish, or Jewish, or Polish and became white in specific relationships with specific groups of people who were not. One of the challenges I offer European-American students is to figure out in relation to whom their family took on this identity. For Scandinavians in Minnesota, it was most likely the Ojibwe; for the Irish and the Jews is was African Americans; for settlers in the Southwest it was both indigenous and Mexican peoples who defined their whiteness; in California it was most likely a mixture of Mexican, Chinese and Native Americans. For all their weight in our lives, the racial categories that define how injustice will be measured out are very circumstantial.

I was excited to see that a recent student strike at the University of Massachusetts at Amherst demanding recruitment, retention, services and academic courses geared toward students of color also included a demand for Irish-American studies. The participation of Irish-American students in a coalition of people of color is a reversal of choices made 150 years ago when the Irish-American community was persuaded to abandon abolitionist sympathies and slave-servant alliances in exchange for a grudging admission into the fraternity of whiteness and other dubious benefits.

If we can teach the history of racism in the United States as the history of the shifting needs of empire, as a history of both impositions and choices, alliances and betrayals, a history with roots far outside and long before the first colonial encounters, if we can hold the tension between disbelief in race and belief in what racism does to us, we will enable more and more young people to remake old and seemingly immutable decisions about where their interests lie and with whom.

Notes

1. Japanese economic competition, particularly in the auto industry, has also brought an increase in popular racism and violence against Asian Americans.

Nevertheless, the image of Asian Americans as a "model minority," as the people of color most likely to do well in school, particularly in technical fields, is a very different stereotype from those imposed on 19th-century and early-20th-century Chinese and Japanese laborers. This is not to say that it's an improvement, only that racism responds to the economic realities of the moment.

Puerto Ricans and Jews

~*1*~

Puerto Ricans and Jews have a long and complex history, but unlike the history of Black-Jewish relations, there has been very little in the way of public discussion of the nature or meaning of our relationship. It is a history that is bound up with the expulsion of the Jews of Spain, the persistent anti-Semitism of the Catholic Church and the Inquisition's persecution of converso Jews in the Americas. It is a history made in the garment sweatshops filled first by Eastern European Jews and then by Puerto Ricans, in times of both solidarity and betrayal, when the price of upward mobility for Jews was the abandonment of people of color. It is a story about the intertwining and confusion of ethnicity and class, about how the acquisition of "whiteness" by immigrant Europeans looked like safety; about how the relatively small, local class privileges of landlord, shopkeeper, employer, insignificant in the larger scale of national and international power, are where the most intimate cruelties of class are visible to the poor, and how ancient Jew-hating mythologies laid blame on the boss, not for being a boss, but for being a Jewish boss. It is also the story of labor struggles fought together, of radical newspapers and shared prison cells, of schoolrooms, neighborhoods and workplaces where Yiddish and Spanish entered each other's homes, and thousands of Judorican marriages and babies were made. This essay is not that history, only a suggestion of some places to look for it, some perspectives to take, an invitation to my peoples to do the work.

~2~

For Puerto Ricans, as for all Latin Americans, the eight centuries of relatively tolerant Moslem rule in southern Spain, the Christian reconquest of the peninsula and the subsequent violent persecution of both Moslems and Jews are a largely unexamined part of our inheritance. Steeped in mythologies of "pure" Spanish culture and blood, we were never taught how newly minted such a notion was in 1492, or how much the Spanish portion of our Latin American identities is owed to Arab and Berber and Jewish civilizations. A real assessment of the history of Puerto Rican-Jewish relations has to begin by examining the relationships that were already in place between Christian and Jewish residents of Iberia long before 1492.

Jews have traditionally worked as tradespeople, mostly small-scale merchants dealing in spices and wines, clothing and food. Often ownership of land was, if not prohibited outright, as risky a proposition as it was for Black farmers in the post-emancipation South—an open challenge to the exclusive rights of an ethnic elite. Continuously in danger of expulsion, Jews gravitated toward the portable, to the movable assets, toward the necessary occupations whose practitioners could buy favors from rulers. With our finances based primarily in trade rather than croplands, Jews were the local providers of credit, from the small-scale loan of goods to be paid from the next harvest eventually to those wealthy merchant bankers who ransomed their communities by extending major loans to kings and queens.

Spanish Jews had enjoyed relative serenity under Moslem rule in Spain, particularly under the earlier regimes. But the North African Almohads who gained control of Moslem Spain in the early 12th century were zealots, bent on the purification of Islam. Their rule saw the only serious repression against Jewish and Christian communities. At the same time, anti-Semitism was on the rise in the Christian-controlled Gothic north. The First Crusade, passing through neighboring France in 1097, resulted in the deaths of thousands of French Jews, massacred as enemies of true religion. In 1182 the blood libel, the myth that Jews sacrificed Christian babies and used their blood to make Passover matzoh, appeared in the Spanish city of Saragossa. Pogroms, violent riots against Jewish communities, often resulting in the murders of many individual Jews, erupted in Spain in times of economic hardship, plagues and other calamities, and the smouldering class resentments of the poor were often directed, not at the lords of the land, but against Jewish merchants and tradespeople.

In 1348, following the appearance of the plague in Aragon, there were massacres of Jews in Saragossa, Barcelona and other Catalonian cities, which spread across Spain. In 1391, at a time of economic crisis, a mob in Seville attacked the Jewish quarter, killing thousands. The pogrom spread to Cordoba, across Andalucía and into the wool-producing cities of the north. There were anti-Jewish riots in Toledo, Madrid, Burgos and Logroño. The Jewish quarters of Barcelona, Valencia and Palma de Mallorca were looted and tens of thousands of Jews died, with many more forced to convert or sold into slavery.

As Christian nobles retook parts of Spain long under Moslem rule, Jewish businesses were seen as rivals to the new enterprises of Christians. Fueled by long-standing religious intolerance, the expulsions and killings of Jews were often also motivated by very direct economic gain. The stereotypes of Jews as unnaturally successful financiers, diabolically greedy and ruthless, stem in part from this competition. Many Jews were in fact poor, their trade consisting of owning small stores of nonperishable goods, or making anything from buttons to shoes. Many others were professionals—doctors, midwives, apothecaries, teachers, scientists and artists employed by the wealthy and powerful. When the Jews were expelled, Spain lost skilled laborers, artists and scholars, health workers and others scientists.

What Puerto Ricans inherit from this history is ignorance about the true place of Jews in Spanish society, ancient prejudices and suspicions, and a belief that Jews are especially exploitative and greedy. In the sixth grade, my English teacher, Miss Rivera, trained at the Catholic teacher's college in Ponce, told our class that Jews get up every morning, spit on our money and then count it. She had never, to her knowledge, met a Jew in her life until my mother's angry note made her realize that one of her favorite students was one. In Barrio Rubias of Yauco where we went to school, the children called me and my brother "moros," because we were unbaptized. Unaware of the irony of that centuries-old term being applied to Jews—our schoolmates egged us on to desecrate homemade crosses so they could find out whether it was true that lightening would strike the child who did such a thing. They had no notion of what it meant to be Jewish, only that we were not Christians. When my parents first arrived in Puerto Rico in the early 1950s, the local Episcopal priest told his congregation that we were Diana worshipers.

~3~

The people who settled Puerto Rico from Spain in the early years of the colonization came from many parts of an Iberia just barely, and still tenuously, united under the domination of Castile and León. Although "new Christians," converted under duress from Judaism or Islam, were not supposed to enter the colonies, clearly the New World was a good place to be headed for New Christians in Spain. In the late 1400s, according to a book on the Inquisition in Santo Domingo, a brother and sister with the surname Morales were brought to trial, denounced by the bishop of Puerto Rico for being suspected judaizers, converts who secretly continued to practice Judaism. In Catholic ideology, judaizers were seen as more dangerous than open Jews because they were more liable to confuse and corrupt Christians. The Morales siblings were accused of desecrating the cross, in this case, hanging a crucifix on the wall and throwing things at it, which seems pointless, dangerous and unlikely. The sister was burned at the stake in Santo Domingo. The brother survived, only to die at the stake in Mexico in 1528.

Researching converso history is made extremely difficult by the fact that Jewish ancestry was something to hide. While some last names are known to be Sephardic in origin, many conversos adopted the names of their sponsors upon conversion. In the records of the Inquisition on Mallorca, certain surnames come up repeatedly in examinations of those under suspicion of being secret Jews, indicating that at least some people of those families were originally Jewish. Among them are familiar immigrant names like Arnau, Alberti, Coll, Moya, Corretjer, Bonet, Janer, Juliá, Alemañy, Barceló, Nadal, Martí, Andreu, Muñoz, Picó, Llorens, Lopez, Perez and Torres. Less common, but still familiar, are Roig, Pelligrí, Ferrer, Prats, Domenech, Oliver, Soler, Noguera and Pons. And these are only the names from Mallorca, not those from Andalucía, where large numbers of Jews lived and where many early immigrants to Puerto Rico came from.

In addition to the conversos and secret Jews who may have come to the Caribbean as direct immigrants, many Spanish Jews first emigrated to Portugal, only to be expelled from that country a few years later. Portuguese converso merchant families were active in the spice trade and probably in slave trading. As Portugal became more and more dangerous for them, they scattered to places where they had existing business ties, in the Mediterranean and part of the Caribbean. According to one historian, the term *portugués* actually came to be a euphemism for converso merchants operating in the Caribbean.

Because the research has not been done, it is impossible to assess the real impact of open Jews, conversos and their Christian descendants on Puerto Rican society. But any real understanding of contemporary relations between our peoples needs to begin with the deep roots of anti-Semitism in Spain and its American colonies.

~4~

There were never very many Jews in Puerto Rico, but when Puerto Ricans began arriving in New York in significant numbers, there was a large Jewish community already in place. Although it included Sephardic Jews like cigar worker Silvestre Breshman, in whose home Cuban and Puerto Rican patriots met, it was overwhelmingly composed of Eastern European, Yiddish-speaking Ashkenazi Jews. In the early years of the century, most Jews worked in working-class occupations and lived in working-class immigrant neighborhoods. Their contacts with Puerto Ricans took place in cigar and garment workshops, in union meetings, in the streets and buildings and schools they shared.

But as many more Jews became upwardly mobile and poor Puerto Ricans arrived in large numbers from the island, Jews were increasingly in positions of privilege in relation to Puerto Ricans: landlords, school teachers, union officials, employers, neighborhood business owners, bank officers, small-scale lenders. In spite of persistent anti-Jewish quotas in education, and discrimination in housing and some areas of employment, significant numbers of Jews were gaining access to the middle class, while Puerto Ricans did not.

Jews were employing a traditional strategy of seeking (mostly moderate) class privilege as a shield against anti-Semitism, a choice that meant abandoning class-based alliances with non-Jews. In a pattern repeated in Europe for centuries, the white Protestant elite used Jews as despised agents, middle persons, buffers. Just as my Lithuanian Jewish ancestors were given land in the Ukraine as a kind of living insulation against Turkish invasion; just as Eastern European Jews were employed to collect taxes from hungry Christian peasants who could have been potential allies against the aristocracy, so in the United States, Jews were being offered conditional privileges of "whiteness," with greater access to upward mobility, in exchange for abandoning alliances with other oppressed groups, particularly people of color.

~5~

While some Jews accepted this option early on, many did not. During the first three decades of the 20th century, many Jews were strongly active in a multi-ethnic labor movement and in anarchist, socialist and communist organizing that prioritized identification with the poor and working classes across cultural lines. While racism did affect the thinking of people in these movements, it is also true that they actively embraced anti-racist causes, standing against lynching and other racist violence, anti-immigrant bigotry, segregation and discrimination of all kinds. The Communist Party, for instance, provided one of the few venues under segregation where Black and white intellectuals could meet and talk politics, and the Party generated and supported many interracial couples.

In 1933, ILGWU organizer Rose Pesotta, herself a Jewish immigrant from Russia, spent months organizing Mexican women garment workers in Los Angeles. Her preconceptions were stereotyped, assuming that Mexican women would be passive, intimidated by the sexism of Mexican men, and therefore hard to organize. While she did face difficulties, they were not as great as expected and her campaign had some significant successes. She came to rely on Mexican women as the backbone of her West Coast organizing and took the male leadership down to the local jails so they could hear the spirit with which the mexicanas sang from their cells.

The following year she went to Puerto Rico to organize women garment workers there. The meetings were full, although women often fainted from hunger while she spoke. She began bringing baskets of food to the meetings and would ask before she spoke if anyone had not eaten. She was deeply moved by the circumstances of Puerto Rican women workers and continued to speak about their living and working conditions for many years. In 1944 she wrote several articles about poverty and working conditions in Puerto Rico for New York newspapers.

The history of New York Jewish and Puerto Rican activism is full of personal and political relationships between our communities. Puerto Rican writer and organizer Jesus Colón, whose second wife, Clara, was Jewish, lived next door to my aunt Eva Levins, and both were active in the Communist Party. In 1943, one month after Jewish partisans in the Warsaw ghetto rose up against the Nazis and managed to drive them from the ghetto, Colón wrote a column in a Spanish-language newspaper, criticizing anti-Semitism in the Latino community.

My own parents also met in the Communist Party. My father's Jewish family had come at the turn of the century from the Ukraine and Byelorussia, both for economic reasons and to evade the draft. Most of them became garment workers. My mother's Puerto Rican parents arrived in New York in 1929 and my grandmother also did garment work, while my grandfather did various janitorial and stock clerk jobs until he was recruited into the electrician's union apprenticeship program during World War II. My mother was taken to her first Communist Party meeting by a Jewish schoolmate in college, while my father's family were longtime activists.

In 1950, Rosa Collazo and Ethel Rosenberg met in prison. Collazo writes about their conversations in the "living room" area near their cells; while Ethel knitted sweaters for her sons, they speculated on whose case was more serious, and which of them, the Communist Jew or the Puerto Rican nationalist was more likely to be executed. These anecdotal encounters show that there was, in spite of class tensions, racism and anti-Semitism, an area of common ground in which progressive people from both communities moved.

~*6*~

In the late '40s and the '50s as the emotional impacts of the Holocaust, the McCarthy persecutions and the establishment of the state of Israel made themselves felt, many formerly liberal, and even progressive Jews retreated politically and sought security in upward mobility and conventional professional lives, and this conventionality included varying degrees of acceptance of economic injustice and racism.

Meanwhile, Puerto Ricans were arriving from the island in record numbers and, in poverty, moving into the same economic slots—in fact, the same neighborhoods—that Jews were moving out of. Puerto Rican women became sweatshop workers in a garment industry where Jews were now among the owners and managers. The ILGWU bureaucracy was largely Jewish men, responsible for representing the interests of Puerto Rican women workers. Jews had won some access to education, even though quotas limited the numbers of Jewish students at universities well into the late '60s, and many were public school teachers. Some played extremely important roles in democratizing the school curricula, pushing for multicultural content and responsiveness to community needs. Others resisted and resented the demands of the new immigrant population for community control and bilingual education.

Puerto Ricans coming from the island had little experience of Jews and were generally steeped in the anti-Semitism of the Catholic Church. Their experiences of class differences, combined with racism, made it easy to accept anti-Semitic stereotyping about all Jews being rich and in control. While Jews were still excluded from the places of genuine power and control, at the level of the barrio, Jews did represent local wealth and power. Puerto Ricans in the barrio never saw the faces of the corporate boards of Citibank or the International Monetary Fund. They saw the landlord, the grocer, the schoolteacher and the pawnshop owner.

Not all of these were Jews. Other immigrant groups like the Italians and the Irish had also acquired both modest class privilege and whiteness, and had a similar kind of power in the barrio. But the perception that Jews were not securely privileged, and did in fact share common interests with people of color, led to bigger expectations and a greater degree of disappointment when Jews behaved in opportunistic ways; and anti-Semitism made it easy to identify class inequities and racism as specific problems of Jewishness.

In recent years, the identification of many U.S. nationalist people of color with Palestinian liberation and the failure of the U.S.-Jewish community as a whole to take a firm stand against racist and colonialist Israeli policies have been added factors in obscuring places of potential alliance. Only by examining fully and honestly the history of our relations can we make decisions about throwing our lot in with each other, not for the short-term gains of opportunism, but for the widest possible vision of our future.

~*Privilege and Loss*

Class, Privilege and Loss

Privilege is both real and unreal. Certainly people live and die because of differences in privilege. At the same time, most of what the privileged think they are getting is illusory. Much of the pursuit of privilege is based on a misconception about what constitutes security. It is based on acquiring material and cultural resources that are denied to others while surrendering integrity, awareness and most of our relationships. Ultimately, privilege is a raw deal.

The acquisition of "whiteness" by various European immigrant groups who were discriminated against and colonized within Europe—for example the Irish and the Ashkenazi Jews—was such an exchange. Both groups were required to surrender vibrant relationships of solidarity with communities of color, specifically African Americans, to betray friends and to accept the mistreatment of those friends as in some way justified. Because of the very insecurity of the privileges offered, both groups were persuaded to narrow their circle of self-interest and accept the exclusion of people of color. White, class-privileged feminists did the same in pursuit of suffrage, sacrificing the liberation of African-American and Native American women, newly immigrant women, poor and illiterate women for the limited rewards of electoral participation.

For a long time I've been interested in finding out what induces people with privilege to give it up or transform it. It never made sense to me that guilt would motivate anyone toward anything lastingly useful. As I traveled around the country working with students who were attempting to tackle issues of racism, class, gender and anti-Semitism, as I worked in a variety of coalitions, in the cultural work and teaching I do, I kept encountering the same desperate refusal of most people to examine the places in their lives where they were privileged. The easier place by far was the place of rage. The high moral ground of the righteously angry victim is in some ways a comforting place, but a place of far greater power is the willingness to examine and dismantle our own privileges and take full responsibility for remaking the world so that neither we nor anyone else can hold it again.

One of those places for me is class. I was raised middle class; my father is a university professor and my mother has mostly worked in our homes, without pay. Several years ago I decided to start a support group for middle-class people who were ready to take on the task of unraveling what being middle class had meant in their lives and figuring out how to really get behind working-class and poor people in concrete ways.

Most middle-class people have working-class ancestors within two generations. Becoming middle class generally means leaving someone behind. For European Americans, becoming white and becoming middle class were often linked, and those left behind included the people of color who defined their whiteness. Underlying the numb self-absorption and unease of many middle-class people is the pain and shame of those old betrayals.

Privilege replaces relationships with things, community with isolated privacy. Leafing through the airline catalogue of knickknacks you can buy from right in your seat, there are machines to rub your neck, rotating pet dishes that will feed your cat during your absence and my favorite, a Styrofoam man marketed to single women, in two available skin colors, with or without legs depending on where you will display him, so that prowlers will not think you are alone. What's more, he comes in a discreet carrying case. Every one of these products is designed to make it unnecessary to have human contact, to ask anyone for help, to have relationships of mutual support. These are the accessories of the cult of individual achievement, neurotic but logical.

The illusion for middle-class people is that the very thin slice of pie we got is worth all the sacrifices. We must pretend that we have arrived, that we have achieved the sum of our desires, that we are secure. But huge as the differences are to those involved, the gap between $8,000 a year and $50,000 is much smaller than the gap between $50,000 and the wealth of the really wealthy. The level of upward mobility available to most of us is meaningless compared with real redistribution. There are people who earn $200 million a year in this country, and that's earned income, not the wealth that just sits around multiplying for its owners. Part of stripping away the illusions of middle-class privilege is looking at real numbers. Naming exactly what we have and where it came from is taboo. Guilt, shame, embarrassment, fear of the envy of others, fear that it isn't really enough and we will be exposed, fear that it's too much and we'll be found out, the notion that it's bad manners, not to have privilege but to talk about it—the pull to hide concrete information about what we have is very strong. And it was incredibly liberating for us to break that taboo, not only about ourselves but about our parents as well. To say, "my father earned $6,000 in rural Puerto Rico in 1965" and hear that someone else's father made $70,000 the same year. To hear that in a room of people who all considered themselves middle class, our income ranged from $14,000 to $100,000.

We are not taught how to take responsibility for the choices involved in privilege, because there are some choices no-one can stand to acknowledge having made. At the same time, we know that people who didn't make these choices, often because they weren't offered the opportunity, didn't always survive. Taking responsibility doesn't mean volunteering to go under. My grandfather literally worked himself to death at the age of forty-six to get his wife and sons into the middle class. Upward mobility was the heroic effort of working-class people to find personal solutions for huge economic disparities. It's one of those compromises with the overwhelming reality of oppression that seems like the only option and costs much more than we think.

When I say that privilege has a cost, I am often met with outrage. Sometimes the anger of the oppressed has no room for this. But if privilege is really the best thing out there, if there are no drawbacks to having it, if no-one in their right mind would exchange it for community, then what on earth do we think we're doing? To expose the fraudulent promises of privilege also frees us from the part of our anger that is envy. In no way does it deny that it is better to eat than to starve. It simply says that to eat abundantly when others are hungry is toxic. Modest meals for everyone are better for everyone.

How to responsibly dismantle our own privilege, how to acknowledge the injury privilege does to those who have it as well as those who lack it, how to make it clear, to ourselves and to those who have what we do not, that surrendering privilege is ultimately joyful and deeply rewarding, that the real losses happened long ago when the privilege was accepted—these are fundamental questions for a much needed theory of solidarity, of how to reweave the torn fabric of our interdependence.

Nadie la Tiene

Land, Ecology and Nationalism

¿Puedes venderme tierra, la profunda
noche de raíces; dientes de
dinosaurios y la cal
dispersa de lejanos esqueletos?
¿Puedes venderme selvas ya sepultadas, aves muertas,
peces de piedra, azufre
de los volcanes, mil millones de años
en espiral subiendo? ¿Puedes
venderme tierra, puedes
venderme tierra, puedes?
La tierra tuya es mía.
Todos los pies la pisan.
Nadie la tiene, nadie.

Can you sell me the earth, the deep night
of roots, dinosaur teeth and the scattered lime
of distant skeletons?
Can you sell me long-buried jungles, dead birds,
fishes of stone, volcanic sulphur, a thousand
million years rising in a spiral? Can you
sell me land, can you
sell me land, can you?
The land that is yours is mine.
Everyone's feet walk it.
No-one has it, no-one.

—African-Cuban poet Nicolas Guillen,
from "¿Puedes?"

~1~

Spring 1995. I sit on the shoulder of our family mountain, one of the highest in this part of the Cordillera Central of Western Puerto Rico, in the pine forest that rises abruptly off the smooth deforested slope to the east, making a profile easy to recognize from miles away. From the red forest floor I look out between the straight trunks of Honduran pine over rolling miles of cleared land planted in bananas, coffee, oranges and drenched alternately in full tropical sunlight and the quick moving rain showers of the season. Each time my brother Ricardo or I return to this farm where we spent our most important childhood years, we make a pilgrimage to this exact place where, after the fire in the early '60s, the forestry service paid our family to plant pine seedlings. They wanted to start a small timber seed industry and our farm became part of the test acreage. In fact, it was Lencho Perez who planted the trees, not us. Hundreds of seedlings in black plastic bags spaded into the blackened hillside. Lencho had been doing odds and ends of agricultural and other work for my parents for several years. In the midst of the Korean war my communist parents called the land "Finca la Paz," peace farm, but Lencho called it "Monte Bravo"—fierce mountain.

In 1966, my father was denied tenure at the University of Puerto Rico where he had been teaching biology. As a professor, he had taken an active part in the 1965 student protests against the war. His unpaid teaching of Marxism and organizing, his trip to Cuba the previous winter, his egalitarian and innovative teaching of biology in a stodgy department lost him his job. My father was essentially blacklisted from teaching on the island, my mother wanted to go back to school and both my parents were concerned about my approaching adolescence in a rural community with inadequate education and a high rate of pregnancy among my friends. So my father accepted a job in Chicago and we moved there.

The day we left, the pine trees were still spindly seven-foot saplings but somehow the knowledge of how they grew without us, how the farm continued to flower and decay sustained my brother and me. The memory of it, the smells and sounds and colors, was one buoyant piece of driftwood in the shipwreck of our intense culture shock. We sent our spirits there for imaginary refuge from the harshness of our new lives and invoked it at night so we could sleep among the alien noises of Chicago. I dreamed of walking up the path into the farm every night for years.

Now we return to it as if checking on a buried treasure. Our ownership of these thirty-four acres preserves the land from clear-cutting, and the fact of that ownership is balm for exile. The colonial economy, the lack of the kind of social and political community we now need, the structures of our personal lives all keep us from coming here to live. But we need the knowledge of that deep valley full of rain, protected from bulldozers. Ownership is a foothold in a slippery place of identity and longing, of necessity and choice.

From my bedroom thousands of miles from here, this piece of earth and the land stretching out around it become a kind of amulet against dispossession. I imagine the rain falling on it, the hawks circling above it, the lizards skittering across it, its continued aliveness an affirmation of my roots there. That in spite of generations of shifting nationalities and loss behind me, in spite of the unpredictable changes of jobs, relationships, rented houses, I have a home on earth. In my imagination the land makes me safe.

But whenever I sit here listening to the wind in the trees, the haunting cry of lizard cuckoos in the valley proclaiming the coming downpour, smell the sunbaked ferns and decaying banana leaves and feel the dense clay under me the symbol begins to unravel. Slowly, as I listen to it, the land becomes itself again. Not mine, not anyone's. Talking to me, yes, but not any more than it talks to the fire ants building their nests or the bats' bones becoming humus or the endlessly chirping reinitas twittering among the señorita flowers.

~2~

I am an ecologist's daughter. I grew up in a house where the permeable boundaries of other worlds criss-crossed our own. At night you could hear the termites munching inside the walls and the slow trickling grains of digested wood. Rats ran in the attic, and if we ventured into the kitchen after hours they stared, offended at our intrusions. Lizards hunted daily on the glass fields of our windowpanes, stalking moths and wasps. Hummingbirds, momentarily stunned from crashing into those windows, would lie in our hands, then shoot back into the hibiscus bushes. Around the ripening bunch of bananas that hung from the kitchen ceiling, clouds of fruit flies rose each time we pulled off a piece of fruit. Autumn evenings of rain, a single tree frog would sing from the moist crevices under the sink. In my parents' bedroom, a long tendril of jasmine that had crept between roof and wall wound sinuously across their shelves of paperbacks. A rat lived inside the washing machine, and my mother always had to hit the side of it before she started it up. It was never our house.

My father would take me walking sometimes, show me the last fading scar of the old road, the Camino Real, poke into the holes of rotten tree trunks, peer into the cups of flowers to see the teeming insect life. I grew up in a place where a tree might fall and within a week, new seedlings sprang from the dead wood. The mountain slid and shifted under the heavy autumn rainfall, the garden left untended grew lush and tangled overnight and it was never the same place for long. How can you own something that changes under your hands, that is so fully alive? Ecology undermines ownership.

~3~

My parents bought this farm for $4,000 in 1951, ninety acres of abandoned coffee plantation that had fallen back into wilderness after the coffee market crash of 1898, the hurricanes of 1899 and 1928 and the economic devastation of Puerto Rico in the '30s and '40s. Near the house I grew up in were the ruins of cement washing tanks and a wide drying platform where we rode our bikes: the last remaining evidence of the coffee boom of the last century when immigrants from Corsica and Mallorca and coastal towns carved up the mountains into land holdings and turned the subsistence farmers who had for centuries cultivated where they pleased into landless laborers. The laborers, the climate and the soil combined to produce the best coffee in the world for wealthy patrons in Paris, Vienna and New York.

When my parents bought it, the coffee had gone wiry, wild ginger choked the pathways and bitter orange, grapefruit and bananas flowered untended under the imported shade trees, brought in to protect the precious crop. My father, unabashedly speaking Brooklyn high school Latin, would stand at the counter of the tiny roadside colmado drinking beers with the coffee laborers until he had enough Spanish to talk politics and begin organizing. My mother used the Agricultural Extension Club to get women out of their houses and learning about leadership and organization at the same time that they learned how to sew, make lard cans into stovetop ovens, cook and do small carpentry projects. After a couple of years my parents sold off half the land at prices the landless or nearly so could afford, and for years people would come around trying to buy from the American who didn't know better. But how else do communists own land?

They raised chickens and the vegetables that my father peddled from their battered red truck. He worked as a lab tech at the hospital in

Castañer and taught in San German while my mother took science courses, farmed, raised me and my brother, washed all the diapers and sheets and work pants by hand, cooked, cleaned and tended the machete wounds and cooking burns of the neighbors at the first aid station. The week my parents were married the Korean War had broken out. They had come to Puerto Rico to await my father's arrest for refusing the draft, uncertain what the consequences would be. But he was declared unfit for service, and they stayed, raised children, made a life and loved the land for its beauty and peace.

~4~

For my ancestors, land had different potency. When Eusebio Morales died in 1802, the lands that were measured for division among his heirs stretched between landmarks like "the old ceiba on the slope above the river." But what lay between those markers was money. Wealth extracted from the land by slave labor and the so-called free labor of the landless. They raised cattle and grew coffee and tobacco, sugar cane and rice. Land and slavery stood behind the petition of Eusebio's grandson Braulio to found a new town, behind the club of wealthy men who rotated among themselves the offices of mayor and militia captain, marrying their children to each other so obsessively that I am descended from the same patriarch by six different lines of descent.

Land and slave holding still stood behind my grandfather in the Depression. When he worked as a janitor and then as a stock clerk in a New York City public school cafeteria. When he fed his family on food the supervisor pretended not to notice he was taking home. It was there in his certainty of his own rightness, in the phrase "por lo derecho" that meant that he lived righteously, with dignity and correctness, not like all those wrong-living títeres that surrounded them in Harlem.

My grandmother Lola expressed that pitying sense of superiority even more overtly than my grandfather. She would speak of some African-American neighbor who was "so nice, poor thing." Although she complained that the Morales' thought her not good enough, her own ancestors had all taken their turns administering class power. It was the service of her ancestors the Díaz brothers leading the local militia against the English invasion of 1797 for which her family was rewarded with lands in Barrio Anones. Although her father had gambled away the family store and she did garment work in New York, although she distanced herself from her relatives and liked the bustling anonymity of New York, she still wore her "buena familia" like an especially nice perfume and was sorry for those who didn't have it, until at the end of her life it became a weapon against the staff of one nursing home after another where she reduced the dark-skinned, working-class workers to angry tears.

~5~

My great-grandfather Abraham Sakhnin also grew up on a farm his family owned. This was in the southern Ukraine, up the railroad line from Odessa. In his old age he painted memories of it: the horses, the cellars full of pumpkins, the harvesting of wheat. The Sakhnins had come from Lithuania in the days of Tsar Nicholas the First when Jews were promised draft exemption if they settled on the borders as a buffer against the Turks. They were given land and taught to farm it by German settlers imported for the task. For five generations they did so. But land, for Jews, in Eastern Europe, was not the foundation it was for Catholic hacendados in Puerto Rico. My great-grandfather fled the farm in 1904 rather than fight in the war against Japan. Pogroms were on the rise along with revolutionary violence, and although the family were Bolshevik sympathizers and some stayed to take part in the revolution, Abe left for Canada and then New York, his first cousin Alter went to Buenos Aires and his sister married and left for Siberia. In 1941 the entire settlement, known as Yaza, was destroyed by Nazis. Land was no guarantee.

~6~

Land is no guarantee, but in the myth-making of exiled and dispossessed nationalisms it becomes a powerful legitimizing force. The central symbol of Puerto Rican nationalism, the phrase most often used to mean that which is struggled for, is "Madre Patria," usually translated as "Mother Homeland." Just as the enthusiastic propagandists of the 1898 U.S. invasion feminized and sexualized the land, describing "her" as well endowed, fruitful and docile, a young girl who "surrenders herself graciously to our virile marines," so, too have nationalists portrayed the colonized country as a captive mother, the "madre tendida en el lecho" (stretched out upon the bed) in the hands of foreigners who rape her.

The idea of "patria" is deeply rooted, like patriotism itself, in both patriarchy and it's raison d'être, patrimony—the inheritance passed from father to son. And the basis of that inheritance is land. Under the rhetoric of "madre patria" lies that which is most despised and exploited in practice, most ignored in nationalist programs, most silently relied on as the foundation of prosperity for the future republic, the basis for its industrial development and for a homegrown class of owners. The unpaid and underpaid labor of women, mothers or not. The labor of agricultural workers so often characterized as "backward sectors." The generous and living land itself. These, in nationalist rhetoric, become purely symbolic sentimental images, detached from their own reality.

Nationalism has tremendous power. It mobilizes just rage about colonial oppression toward a single end. It subordinates all other agendas to that end. It silences internal contradictions among the colonized, postpones indefinitely the discussion of gender, sexuality, class and often "race," endowing nationalist movements with a kind of focused, single-minded passion capable of great force. But although that force draws its energy from the real pain and rage and hope of the colonized, nationalism does not attempt to end all forms of injustice. Nationalism is generally, both in the intent of its leaders and in its results, a one-point program to capture patrimony for a new group of patriarchs.

~7~

In nationalist rhetoric, land does not move. No wonder it is so often portrayed as a mother. Eternal, loyal and patient, it waits for its exiled children to come home. It would know them anywhere. But the real land, the soil and rocks and vegetation, is never still. In the United States the average acre of land loses five tons of soil every year, blown by wind across property lines and fences, municipalities and national borders, washed by rain into river systems that drain a thousand miles downstream. Even massive shapes like the Grand Canyon shift and collapse and move continually. Each autumn in Puerto Rico the water running off our mountain turns a heavy orange and flows away downhill, leaving the silt of our property spread over hundreds of square kilometers of flatlands and leagues of sea.

This movement of land has occasionally been used as part of imperial reasoning. In the late-19th century, one U.S. statesman claimed that Cuba was literally U.S. soil because it must have been formed by mud washing out of the mouth of the Mississippi. But "national soil" is a nonsensical statement. Places have history, but soil does not have nationality. Just as the air we breathe has been breathed by millions of others first and will go on to be breathed by millions more; just as water falls, travels, evaporates, circulates moisture around the planet—so the land itself migrates. The homeland to which Jews claim to have returned (land of the Canaanites before them and many others after) is not the same land. The earth that lay around the Temple could be anywhere by now. So what exactly is it we've been dreaming of for so long?

~8~

Land and blood. Mystical powers that never change their identity so that a speck of Mississippi mud and an individual red blood cell are both seen as carrying unalterable identity, permanent membership in human cultures. This is the mysticism that allows fascist movements to call up images of long-dispersed and recombined ancestral peoples like the ancient Aryans and Romans, or entirely mythic genetic strains like the White Race, and scream for genocide to return them to a state of purity.

The reality is that people circulate like dust, intermingling and reforming, all of us equally ancient on this earth, all equally made of the fragments of long-exploded stars, and if, by some unlikely miracle, a branch of our ancestors has lived in the same place for a thousand years, this does not make them more real than the ones who have continued circulating for that same millennium. All of us have been here since people were people. All of us belong on earth.

So what about the stealing of land? What about all the colonized places on earth? What of indigenous peoples forcibly removed by invaders? The crime here is a deeper and more lasting one than theft, akin in some ways to enslavement. Before land can be stolen, it must become property. The relationships built over time between the land and the human members of its ecosystem must be severed just as ties of family and village and co-humanity were severed so that slavers could enslave. The indigenous peoples of the Americas did not own land in the European sense. They lived with and from the land and counted it as a relative. The blow that cracked Hawaiian sovereignty was the imposition of land ownership. At gunpoint, Hawaiians were forced to divide sacred and common land, to commodify it, price it, allot it. In Europe itself, it was the enclosure of the commons, the grazing lands and great forests from which people subsisted, that created a massive class of landless laborers to fill the factories and transport the goods of industrial capitalism. Earth-centered cultures everywhere held our kinship with land and animals and plants as core knowledge, central to living. The land had to be soaked with blood and that knowledge, those cultures shattered, before private ownership could be erected. It wasn't just theft.

~9~

And yet owning has seemed like such a good defense. With the common lands gone, strive to own. With land commodified and confiscated, struggle to enforce treaties. If you are driven away, fight to return. For Jews, barred for centuries from landholding, how legitimating, how healing, what a chance to strike back at history it is to acquire land. Why should we alone be excluded? When Baron Rothschild sought to help the Jews of Eastern Europe to escape the pogroms, he bought them land: in Argentina, in New Jersey, in other places, and settled them there to farm. Landlessness had been a central feature of Jewish oppression. Having land became a symbol of resistance. Our own connections with land have been severed time after time. We would come to know and trust a particular landscape, to understand Babylonian weather, to know the growing seasons of Andalucía, to recognize the edible wild foods of the woods around Rouen, the wildflowers on the Dneiper or the Rhine or the Thames, and it would be time for another hurried departure. To have land, to farm became one of the most emotionally powerfully images of Jewish freedom, even when getting land meant severing someone else's ties to it. Even when it meant tearing the olive trees and the fragrant dust and the taste of desert spring water out of the lives of Palestinians whose love for the land was hundreds of generations deep.

In the 1930s my father's family sang this song, translated from the Yiddish of Russian Jews:

> On the road to Sebastopol,
> not so far from Simfaropol
> Just you go a little further on.
> There you'll see a collective farm,
> run by sturdy Jewish arms
> and its called Zhankoye, Zhan.
> Aunt Natasha drives the tractor,
> Grandma runs the cream extractor
> as we work we all can sing this song:
> Who says Jews cannot be farmers?
> Spit in his eye who would so harm us.
> Tell him of Zhankoye, Zhan.

~10~

Land ownership was only a hundred years old in my community of Indiera when I was growing up. Its hold on people's imaginations was still tenuous. It was not until the 1860s that the Massinis and Nigaglionis, Agostinis and Pachecos began filing title claims to large stretches of mountain lands. That there were already people living on and from that land was irrelevant, because none of them had surveyed it, fenced it, paid a lawyer to draw up deeds to it. Since at least the 1570s, the mountains had been worked by wandering subsistence farmers who would clear and burn off a bit of forest, cultivate it for a few years and move on while the land renewed itself. Descendants of Arawak and other indigenous people enslaved by the Spanish, runaway slaves and poor Europeans, the people of the mountains didn't own the land. They moved across it and lived from it.

The new settlers owned and profited. Our own farm was carved out by a Corsican named Massari who, like the others, planted the new boom crop, arabiga coffee, for faraway markets. Then it was owned by Pla who was Mallorcan. Then by my parents. But the neighbors who held small plots and worked other people's land for cash never seemed to take boundaries seriously the way my neighbors in New England did. Everyone harvested bananas, root vegetables, oranges and wood from the farms of the Canabals, the Nigaglionis, or Delfín Rodriguez who only kept Hacienda Indiera as a tax writeoff to protect his sugar profits. Our neighbor to the north, Chago Soto, was always moving the fence between our properties. On one visit we found that Cheito Agostini had built pens for his pigs on our side of the road. Another time, exploring the deep overgrown valley on the back side of our land, my sister-in-law and I stumbled across a cement holding tank built over one of the springs and plastic pipes leading the water out to a house and garden. It was only when we introduced ourselves to the man loading a truck in front of the house and saw his chagrin that we realized that the water was on our side of the property line.

So what do communist landholders do with privilege? My father says you have to get rid of it or use it for the common good. So we tell Cheito he can keep the pigs there, but no more dumping piles of Pampers, and no permanent structures. We let the farmer to the north know that we understand the water came from our land, and for now it's OK. But what are we doing with this land at all, now that we don't live there?

~11~

Class privilege allows us this option: to see ourselves as stewards of this land. Because we don't need to live from these thirty-four acres, we can resist the pressure to sell. Our neighbors keep asking: can't you sell us a piece of the farm to expand my coffee, my bananas, to build a house? After all, you're not using it. Poverty does not allow them the luxury of thinking twenty or thirty years ahead, but we know the land they want now for farming cash crops will pass through their hands and into other uses and that in thirty years this place would be lots for cement houses. My mother says the rich ruin the poor and the poor ruin the land.

From up here in the cordillera you can see where the rich ruin land directly. We grew up with the smudge of poisoned air over Guayanilla, where the oil refineries used to make such a stench we would always buy sweet maví to drink before we got there so we could hold the cups over our noses as we went by. There are puffs of dust where the limestone hills are being bulldozed and ground into cement for more housing developments, shopping malls, factories. So much of the land has been paved, in fact, that the drenching rains of autumn have nowhere to soak in. The water runs off into the sea now, and the water table has dropped so much that last year some neighborhoods in San Juan went without water for weeks at a time. But up here it hasn't yet been worth the developers' while. Here it's the desperation they've created in the lives of the poor that does the work for them.

Between the land hunger of the poor to turn acreage into a little money and the commodification of the earth into real estate, only privilege seems able to preserve the land. The Rockefellers, buying up islands, keep pockets of wildness alive in the Caribbean while deforestation and massive shopping malls destroy the freshwater supplies of Puerto Rico, leaving everyone thirsty.

This is what we want our privilege to buy, my brothers and I. Because of how we lived there, because of the ways our parents cherished and nurtured our intimacy with the land, we know we're kin to it. We don't want it to die. But we also want to give the land a chance to tell its story and the story of the people who have worked it. On that overgrown abandoned coffee farm in the middle of increasingly cleared and pesticide-soaked lands, we want to build a cultural center and museum of the history and ecology of Indiera, where the community can participate in retelling its past. We hope that in this process of storytelling, the people of Indiera will rediscover pride in their heritage of work and a new sense of their connection to this land. By drawing tourist dollars from the nearby Panoramic Highway, we also want to model another way of living from the land, in which livelihood comes not from extracting the land's wealth but from telling, in as much detail as we can, the complex story of our relations with it.

I imagine a museum filled with family photographs, letters from migrant children who moved away, and recorded voices of elders testifying. I imagine showing the people who grow coffee the faces of the people who drink it and vice versa. I imagine a narrow pathway winding down into the rain valley through the forest of tree ferns, South American shade trees, wild guavas and African Tulip trees. I remember how my father used to take his microscope down to the schoolhouse and how the children would crowd around waiting for a turn to be amazed at what the world looks like close up. I imagine the children of the barrio walking among the photographs and voices and trees that way, renaming their place on this land and in the world.

~12~

Because the land is alive, our relationship with it is real. We are all kin to the land, love it, know it, become intimate with its ways, sometimes over many generations. Surely such kinship and love must be honored. Nationalism does not honor it. Nationalism is about gaining control, not about loving land. But it wears the cloak of that love, strips it from its sensual and practical roots and raises it into a banner for armies. The land invoked as a battle cry is not the same land that smells of sage, or turns blue in the dusk, or clings thickly to our boots after rain. That land is less than nothing to the speech makers.

The land invoked to the beating of nationalist drums is what lies at the linguistic roots of the term "real estate," meaning royal property. It is the land my hacendado forebears kept in the bank, ransacked, used to pay the bills. The land bristling with "No Trespassing" signs, the land the lords of Europe enclosed against the peasants in the infancy of capitalism, the land as symbol of power over. It is the land we can be mobilized to recapture because, with its fences and mortgages and deeds, it has been the symbol of our dispossession.

~13~

Ownership shatters ecology. For the land to survive, for us to survive, it must cease to be property. It cannot continue to sustain us for much longer under the weight of such merciless use. We know this. We know the insatiable hunger for profit that drives that use and the disempowerment that accommodates to it. We don't yet know how to make it stop.

But where ecology meets culture there is another question. How do we hold in common not only the land, but all the fragile, tenacious rootedness of human beings to the ground of our histories, the cultural residues of our daily work, the individual and tribal longings for place? How do we abolish ownership of land and respect people's ties to it? How do we shift the weight of our times from the single-minded nationalist drive for a piece of territory and the increasingly barricaded self-interest of even the marginally privileged toward a rich and multi-layered sense of collective heritage? I don't have the answer. But I know that only when we can hold each people's particular memories and connections with land as a common treasure can the knowledge of our place on it be restored.

Acknowledgements

I've wanted to write some version of this essay for years. Thanks to Ruth Atkin for asking me to do so. As is often the case with me, during the writing of this piece, I had extensive conversations with my mother, Rosario Morales, and my father, Richard Levins. They contributed clarity, insights and factual detail about our farm and their own histories. Thanks to my father for talking about the legitimacy of a wandering heritage, his comments on the mysticism of blood and soil and for always sharing with me his love of history and his delight in ecological and historical complexity. Thanks to my mother for her clearheadedness, her sharp nose for bad politics and for our ongoing discussions of feminism and nationalism, class, writing and everything else. Thanks to them both for deciding to have me and then my brothers "so we would have someone to talk to." They continue to be my closest political, intellectual and artistic companions.

Glossary

colmado	small grocery/general store
por lo derecho	literally: on the straight path, living the right way.
buena familia	"good family," meaning families with longstanding privilege
títere	somewhere between brat and hoodlum.

Torturers

Several years ago the media was full of the story of two ten-year-old English boys who had beaten a toddler to death. The coverage dripped with revulsion and hatred toward these children. They were described as inhuman, as evil, as bad seed. Reporters exclaimed, enraged, that they showed no remorse and wished aloud that there was a death penalty for ten-year-olds. The complete rejection of the boys couldn't be said often, or loudly or vehemently, enough. They are not of us. We are not like them. If we don't destroy them, we will never be safe. What I didn't hear anyone ask was what had to happen to a pair of children that by the age of ten they could batter another child to death with a brick.

Torturers are made, not born. We know enough about the repetitive cycles of violence, enough about the training of secret police and death squads, special military units and spies, to know that the way you learn to torture is through torture. As a child I had an intimate view of this process. For a period of several years, without the knowledge of my parents, I was periodically abused by a small group of adults who practiced physical, psychological and sexual tortures, mostly, though not exclusively, on children. It was clear that their treatment of me had several goals. They deliberately confused and intimidated me so I would not reveal what was happening, but they also were attempting to reproduce themselves in me and the other children, to separate us from our own humanity enough to turn us into torturers as well.

Because I was already a highly politicized child by the time they got hold of me, because I already knew about political torture and resistance to it, I was able to develop a strategy that defeated them. They managed to keep me from telling, but I did not continue the cycle of abuse. I figured out that I was powerless to prevent what they did to my body but that I could safeguard my spirit. I understood that the first step in becoming like them was to learn to dehumanize others and that part of the goal of their cruelty was to make us hate them, make us want to hurt them, make us see them as monsters we would be willing to torment. To plant in us the seeds of their own pain.

Part of the way I prevented this was to envision my abusers as young children, before they became this cruel. I would imagine that imprisoned within the adult bodies that hurt me were captive children who had themselves been tortured. I would pretend I could catch their eyes, send them signals of solidarity to give them courage. Imagine how horrified they were at the actions of their grown-up selves. This was what enabled me to survive spiritually.

This experience, and the stories I have heard from other survivors of torture, whether sponsored by governments or groups of individuals, has left me with a sense of urgency to understand how children grow up to be torturers and how torturers sometimes, often suddenly, become incapable of continuing to torture.

This is a critical question for a number of reasons. Obviously, if we can figure out how to stop the reproduction of torture, the world will be a safer place for all of us. But it is also true that if we have nothing but retribution to offer the perpetrators of the world, we will, in an important sense, become like them. We cannot hold out a political vision of a compassionate world, inclusive and just, and reject their wounded humanity. The urge to punish, to execute, to wipe them out is the refusal to consider what we ourselves might be capable of. We try to move the toxic wastes of oppression from site to site, exiling the mercenaries and dictators, imprisoning the human rights violators, convicting the war criminals and sealing them in supposedly leak-proof containment vessels. The toxicity remains.

I speak for the torturers because they are the tortured who did not survive intact. I speak for the ones who were so numbed by the world they saw and the part they were told to play in it that they cannot understand the reality of the harm they do. Of the men who tortured me, I wrote:

> There are people in this world
> so terrified that they hunger, night and day, for the fear of others.
> There are people in this world
> who can show their wounds only by inflicting them,
> and the story of my body
> is also the map of their unspeakable pain.

To me the choice seems difficult and clear. Either we are committed to making a world in which all people are of value, everyone redeemable, or we surrender to the idea that some of us are truly better and more deserving of life than others, and once we open the door to that possibility, we cannot control it. If we are willing to say that some people don't matter, that some people are unaffordable for the planet, that some people's actions have placed them beyond the pale, then what forgiveness is there for any of us, if we commit errors, even crimes? If we agree to accept limits on who is included in humanity, then we will become more and more like those we oppose. Do we really need to name the list of atrocities committed by people who claimed to act in the name of human liberation?

Salvadoran poet Roque Dalton wrote, "Altogether they have more death than we, but altogether we have more life than they." For this to be true, we must hold a larger vision of what is possible than the people who kill and torture and ravage. In her remarkable novel *The Fifth Sacred Thing*, Starhawk explores the challenge of this choice in depth. The future egalitarian community of San Francisco must devise a strategy of resistance against remorselessly brutal armies from a nightmare South characterized by corporate wealth, fanatically bigoted religion and extremes of social control. Having principles is easy when not much is at stake. The dilemma Starhawk presents her characters with is much harder. How is it possible to face violence strong enough to destroy all that you love and not become corrupted by it? The strategy of the elders is twofold: to face the invaders with the human consequences of their actions and to continually invite them to abandon the role of abuser and rejoin humanity. One of the characters says, "We will have victory only if we are stronger healers than they are warriors."

A fully just society in which human potential is never despised or thrown away is only possible if that invitation is always open. There is nothing more moving to me than the stories of people who had the courage to reclaim their humanity even after full participation in the shameful. Too few people know that the beautiful hymn "Amazing Grace" was written in gratitude by a slave trader who suddenly, mid-Atlantic, awoke to the horror of what he was doing and refused to participate any further. Like the slave trader, what often breaks the numbness of the perpetrator and enables him to make a new choice is being confronted with the real consequences of his actions, glimpsing the humanity of those he is hurting.

One of the consequences of oppression is that it is morally corrupting, not only for those who exercise power over others, but also for those who are rendered powerless. The fewer options for effective action we see for ourselves, the easier it becomes to narrow our understanding of our best interests and justify sacrificing others; and prolonged captivity often leaves the captive with an urge to please the captor. For instance, it was often other slaves who betrayed the plans for escapes or rebellions to the slave masters, parts of the Latino community support anti-immigrant legislation that distinguishes them from undocumented newcomers, and Roque Dalton died at the hands of a rival faction of the Salvadoran left. All of us have had failures of integrity. I believe part of what makes it so hard to consider perpetrators as part of our constituency is that we cannot bear to examine the ways in which we resemble them. Until we confront the moments when we have been co-opted, coerced or seduced into harming others, we will be vulnerable to becoming defensively self-righteous. Like those English reporters, we will exclaim in horror over the crimes without taking responsibility for the world that keeps turning children into criminals.

What am I calling for is not a liberal policy of forgiving and forgetting, nor the public relations maneuver of mass pardons and political absolutions—no starting from scratch. I am holding out for a radical refusal to compromise on the possibility of any one of us to heal, make new moral choices, make amends and reclaim kinship with those we have harmed.

There is a place for righteous rage at the torturers, and a place to demand accountability and hard work. But punishment is not a tool of liberation; it is the powerless exercise of violence by those who can think of nothing better. It is the refusal to acknowledge our kinship with those who hurt us. It is a laying down of our vision, and ultimately, if we cannot overcome it, our vision, which is what truly distinguishes us from those we oppose, will die.

~Integrity

Radical Pleasure

Sex and the End of Victimhood

~ 1 ~

I am a person who was sexually abused and tortured as a child. I no longer define myself in terms of my survival of this experience, but what I learned from surviving it is central to my political and spiritual practice. The people who abused me consciously and deliberately manipulated me in an attempt to break down my sense of integrity so they could make me into an accomplice to my own torture and that of others. They deliberately and consciously interfered with my sexuality as one method of accomplishing this. We are so vulnerable in our pleasures and desires. The fact they could induce physical pleasure in me against my will allowed them to shame me. It allowed them to persuade me that my sexuality was untrustworthy and belonged to others. It allowed them to persuade me that my desires were dangerous and were one of the causes of my having been abused. My sexuality has stuttered ever since, flaring and subsiding in ways I have not known how to manage, ricocheting from intense excitement to absolute numbness, from reckless trust to impenetrable guardedness. This place of wounded eroticism is one that is honored in survivor culture, evidence of blows inflicted and then denied by our abusers. When the skeptical ask us "Where are your scars?" we can point to the unsteady rhythms of fascination and disgust, obsession and revulsion through which we experience sex as evidence of what we know to be true.

~2~

"So why choose to reclaim sex?" This is the final question in a five-hour interview of me by my friend Staci Haines. We have been talking about the seductiveness of the victim role; about the thin satisfactions that come from a permanent attitude of outrage. About how having to resist too much, too young, locks us into rigid stances of resistance that interfere with intimacy, which ultimately requires vulnerability and surrender. About the seductiveness of an identity built on righteous indignation, and how close that stance actually lies to rampant self-pity. So when she asks me "Why reclaim sex?" I answer in layers.

Of course because it is part of aliveness. But among the many topics we've ranged over in our hours of conversation, the one that grabs me now is the need and obligation to leave victimhood behind. Staci and I share a somewhat taboo belief that as survivors we have an obligation to think about the healing of the perpetrators who are, after all, our kin—victims who survived in body but were unable to remain spiritually intact. So what comes to mind is the high price we pay when we settle for being wronged. Victimhood absolves us from having to decide to have good lives. It allows us to stay small and wounded instead of spacious, powerful and whole. We don't have to face up to our own responsibility for taking charge of things, for changing the world and ourselves. We can place our choices about being vulnerable and intimate and effective in the hands of our abusers. We can stay powerless and send them the bill.

But deciding not to heal fully, not to reclaim that place of intimate harm and make it flourish, is also unjust. By making the damage done to us permanent and irreversible, we lock both ourselves and the perpetrators away from any hope of healing. We saddle them with an even bigger spiritual debt than they have already incurred, and sometimes the reason is revenge, as if our full recovery would let them off the hook and we must punish them by seeing to it that our victimhood is never diminished or challenged. But when we refuse healing for the sake of that rage, we are remaking ourselves in the image of those who hurt us, becoming the embodiment of the wound, forsaking both ourselves and the abandoned children who grew up to torment us.

~3~

The path of reclaiming the wounded erotic is neither placid nor boring. It is full of dizzying precipices, heady moments of release, crushing assaults of shame. But at its core is the real fire we are all after, that blazing and untarnished aliveness that lies within everything of value and spirit that we do. Right here in our bodies, in our defense of our right to experience joy, in the refusal to abandon the place where we have been most completely invaded and colonized, in our determination to make the bombed and defoliated lands flower again and bear fruit, here where we have been most shamed is one of the most radical and sacred places from which to transform the world. To shamelessly insist that our bodies are for our own delight and connection with others clearly defies the predatory appropriations of incestuous relatives and rapists; but it also defies the poisoning of our food and water and air with chemicals that give us cancer and enrich the already obscenely wealthy, the theft of our lives in harsh labor, our bodies used up to fill bank accounts already bloated, the massive abduction of our young people to be hurled at each other as weapons for the defense and expansion of those bank accounts—all the ways in which our deep pleasure in living has been cut off so as not to interfere with the profitability of our bodies. Because the closer I come to that bright, hot center of pleasure and trust, the less I can tolerate its captivity, and the less afraid I am to be powerful, in a world that is in desperate need of unrepentant joy.

Circle Unbroken

The Politics of Inclusion

Historically, attempts to create unity across difference have depended, by and large, on the strategy of a lowest-common-denominator goal, with all other agendas and aspirations put on hold. The inevitable result is that when that limited goal is won, this temporary alliance, no matter how powerful it has been in the short run, collapses. The U.S. suffrage movement increasingly focused on the vote as a single issue to which all of women's other needs were subordinated. This policy alienated many women, and once suffrage was achieved, the movement dissipated. Nicaraguans in large numbers could be brought together around a program of removing Somoza, even though there was much less agreement about what to do with the country afterward and how.

Deep-rooted and lasting change needs a broad base of support, and it has become more and more clear to me that any broad and enduring alliance with the goal of radically changing the social structures needs to be based on a different kind of unity. For this purpose, it is no longer useful to keep doing single-oppression theory, to keep defining and elaborating our understandings of the exact nature of racism, sexism, class and sexual orientation as if they ever operated in isolation. In the very beginning stages of a movement, it can be useful for a very short while to concentrate on defining the parameters of a single under-examined power relationship. But the interest and usefulness of this approach wears thin quite rapidly.

My experience of the second wave of feminism in the United States demonstrates this clearly. For a period of five years at most, and that's probably stretching it, it was possible for large numbers of feminists to talk about "women" in a fairly uncomplicated way as we named for ourselves the most discernible features of patriarchy. Of course, what was most discernible varied immensely depending on who was looking, and by the early 1970s lesbians were presenting major challenges to the heterosexism within the women's movement, closely followed, at least in the organizations in which I participated, by women of color exposing the racism that shaped both our agendas and our ways of working. Since that time, more and more constituencies of women have insisted that the particularities of all our lives be central to feminism if it is to have any validity.

What we have discovered is that it is not possible to win large numbers of women to a program of ending patriarchy if what is required is that they leave outside all the other components of their lives—colonialism, class oppression, racism, heterosexism and much more. If they are required to pretend that patriarchy affects all women in the same ways. If they are asked to leave aside the particularities of their lives for a privileged generalization. Only a feminism that is inclusive, that fully integrates the expertise of all women, that does not indulge in a hierarchy of liberation agendas will be capable of bringing large numbers of women together in long-term alliance. Therefore, the theory we need to be developing is one that helps us understand the relationships among our different and multifaceted lives with all their specific struggles and resources. Rather than build unity through simplification, we must learn to embrace multiple rallying points and understand their inherent interdependence.

Such a theory needs to move away from the idea of "intersections" of oppression and assume a much more organic interpenetration of institutional systems of power. Although the intent is to address complexity, the idea of distinct intersecting realities still treats the social categories of "woman," "working class," "lesbian," "person of color," etc., as if it were possible to separate someone's "woman-ness" from her class position, her "racial"/ethnic position and so on. But these social categories do not exist in their "pure" state. Every woman is a woman of some class, some ethnicity, some sexual orientation, some country. The notion that working-class, colonized women of color suffer from "triple jeopardy" has always bothered me, because the implication is that racism and class oppression have no effect on those who are privileged by it. There is no such thing as "single jeopardy." The only way to believe that the -isms are separable is by ignoring privilege—so that upper-class, heterosexual, European and U.S. white women are thought about only in the context of gender, as if they existed only in the categories in which they are oppressed. Social categories don't intersect like separate geometric planes. Each one is wholly dependent on all the others for its existence. For a liberation theory to be useful, it must address the way systems of oppression/privilege saturate each other, are mutually necessary and, in fact, do not exist without one another.

My father, Richard Levins, says that any time progressive causes seem to be in conflict, it's because neither group is asking enough. Because no one has been able to imagine a solution big enough to meet everyone's needs—as when, for example, the employment of loggers and the preservation of forests are pitted against each other in a bitter struggle over which unsatisfactory solution to opt for, but the creation of an economy that preserves both people and trees is outside the parameters of the debate. To organize social change on the basis of all people's real needs, refusing to sacrifice anyone, does not mean conducting 2,000 fragmented campaigns at once. It doesn't mean making sure to add a few clauses in the last paragraph of the speech that mention all the people we "should" include. Such cosmetic inclusion, whether in theory or practice, always looks uncomfortably acrobatic to me—unnecessarily complicated and at the same time evasive. It's a maneuver to preserve that privileged and simplistic worldview that makes inequity tolerable. Real inclusion is both straightforward and intricate, complex and interesting enough to spend a lifetime working for. It just requires that we understand enough about how our lives are entwined that whatever activist task we undertake we figure out how the question we're asking or the particular piece of injustice we're confronting can be made big enough, connected enough, to be useful to everyone. The most useful theory will be that which teaches us to use the particular, to frame big and inclusive questions, to integrate seemingly conflicting needs and sacrifice no one.

To craft a theory that can explain why we mustn't abandon anyone, it is necessary to have an explanation for people's bad decisions that is not based on their having inherent flaws, If we refuse to essentialize people, we need to have a historical explanation for stupid and destructive behavior. For me, the concept of internalized oppression provides the most important insights into the behavior of oppressed people. Seeing how internalized institutional abuse affects people's choices allows me to explain people's actions as separate from their potential—to say that people make the best choices they can at any particular moment. A theory of internalized oppression offers all kinds of strategies for coping with the difficulties of organizing. Without it, people tend to develop exclusive policies. Without the tools to understand and specifically struggle with internalized oppression, the tendency is to define the people who show its impact on them as "defective." Similarly, internalized privilege distorts our capacity to see common interests, notice large areas of social interaction in which we are privileged and others are not, or have a realistic sense of our own role in collaboration with others.

A corollary to internalized oppression as an explanation for behavior that seems to go against our own interests is that we always have agency. All our responses to our conditions are strategic, the best we could come up with at the moment. We are always trying to figure out how best to survive and thrive. Sometimes our ability to accurately assess our situation—the probable impact of our actions, where we are most likely to find reliable support and whose interests lie closest to our own—becomes distorted as we make judgments based on inaccurate expectations of ourselves and others. But we are never simply acted upon. This is critical, especially when we attempt to understand seemingly senseless actions of people whose experience of oppression is significantly different from our own. Unless we understand the complex motivations that lie behind people's decisions, we will be likely to essentialize them in the most patronizing ways, so that the effects of oppression upon them become a justification for continued oppression.

In building a politics of inclusion, we need to map the ways in which our own thinking has been affected by oppression. The process of consciousness raising, of naming the specific ways in which our particular experiences of inequity traumatized us, is an invaluable theorizing tool. There are few things as powerful as identifying the manufacturer's mark on what we have perceived as our personal demons. From this process we can emerge with compassionate respect for our own and each other's creativity in the face of often incomplete and inaccurate information, and extract lessons about what has and hasn't been effective, without needing to shame our earlier selves. This in turn will give us the tools we need to find points of connection with people whose experiences are very different from our own, and whose choices we may be inclined to judge.

Full inclusion requires us to abandon all the places where we have been tricked into collusion with oppression, and all of us have. It requires us to move beyond our comfort zones. I once heard Bernice Reagon say that being in coalition meant working with people we didn't much like, and we might need to vomit over it for while, but we had to do it anyway. Making a politics of inclusion, of integrity, means not only working with those we don't like, but taking responsibility for figuring out in what ways their liberation is bound up with our own, in what way our burning issues can be linked. It means refusing the luxury of self-righteousness, that form of liberalism in the name of radicalism through which we agree to avoid people or issues that we can't stand to think about. It is easy for many leftists to indulge in amused contempt toward movements that don't center on economic injustice or include people whose traumas make them unacceptable. We dissociate ourselves from animal rights activism, "wilderness only" environmentalism, or the liberation movements of transgendered people, mental health system survivors, survivors of extreme sexual abuse. We need to rigorously root out our tendency to patronize or avoid such movements and take charge of finding ways to make the necessary links that will expand the visions of both their movements and our own until we find the point of collaboration.

Solidarity is not a matter of altruism. Solidarity comes from the inability to tolerate the affront to our own integrity of passive or active collaboration in the oppression of others, and from the deep recognition of our most expansive self-interest. From the recognition that, like it or not, our liberation is bound up with that of every other being on the planet, and that politically, spiritually, in our heart of hearts we know anything else is unaffordable.

Walking the Talk,
Dancing to the Music
The Sustainable Activist Life

"If you can talk you can sing. If you can walk you can dance."
South African proverb

"If I can't dance, I won't be part of your revolution."
Emma Goldman

How does one live up to a lifelong activist commitment and not become burned out, cynical, or simply too exhausted to move? Sustainable activism is not simply a matter of organizing energy and applying it to tasks. Anyone can do that in a crisis, in a pinch, for a while. Long-term activism requires more or less reliable, ongoing sources of hopefulness, faith, joy and trust because it is a matter of believing in and working for possibilities that are nowhere in sight. In her play *Twilight: Los Angeles,* Anna Deavere Smith quotes Cornel West on the difference between optimism and hope. Optimism, he says, is when you look around, and see the evidence that things are going well. Hope is when you look around see no evidence at all that things are going well, but continue to act on faith. [1]

This is the kind of faith that long-term activism, spanning decades of ups and downs, requires. It is another one of those acrobatic feats in which we need to find ways to live as if what we want to build were already here. We live in a society that offers us cheap imitations, that devalues the spiritual in favor of consumption or empty religious forms devoid of spirit, that substitutes the individual for the personal and offers us entertainment and addiction instead of living art. And in order to sustain ourselves, in order to fully tap our power to make social change and do the work we want to do in the world, not for the duration of one crisis after another, but for fifty or sixty years, what we need is the restoration of these profound sources of nourishment: connection with spirit, connection with the personal and connection with the creative. Only such a base gives us the flexibility to adapt to changing conditions, to stay hopeful in times of setback, to balance patience and persistence and choose our battles wisely.

The spiritual need not be rooted in religion. But in order for us to weather the times when evidence of forward motion is just not available, we need to have a sense of something much larger than ourselves in which we trust. My father believes in the creativity of people, in their capacity to eventually think their way through a brick wall. He believes in a kind of cumulative creativity that moves history, in which our desire to learn, to find ways that work seeps through the rigid structures meant to contain us. He told me when I was very young that there were no bad people, just bad decisions. That's the kind of faith that allows someone to sit out the bad times, what he calls the trough between waves, knowing a new wave will come.

The spiritual is whatever allows us to notice the miraculous nature of life, how it keeps coming back, asserting itself in the midst of destruction. Whatever allows us to notice that life is in fact bigger than all the mean-spirited cruelties and brutalities of unjust societies. Something large enough to entrust our sense of future to, so that we don't become mired in struggle. People find this in a wide variety of places, from solitude by the ocean to reading history, from trust in God to trust in people, from meditation to gardening, from being with young children to visiting ancient ruins to gazing at stars immeasurably older than any problems we confront. It doesn't seem to matter what the source is, but without some sense of abundance, people get overwhelmed and lose their compassion and good judgment in urgency.

Our society is individualistic to the point of insanity. Concern for the common good is ridiculed as naive, and the skills of people from more communally oriented cultures are seen as liabilities. In the frenetic emphasis on individual achievement we are taught nothing about real purpose, or that there is a relationship between our own satisfaction and the good of the people around us. What is marketed as the personal is an endless array of techniques that attempt to compensate us for our loss of meaningful work and intimate relationships, and they bear the same relationship to a sustaining culture of interdependence that "enriched" white bread pumped full of synthetic vitamins does to a loaf of stone-ground whole wheat.

A false dichotomy between the personal and the social has polarized those who want to renew and reinvent intimacy, and attempt to reverse some of the profound alienation that oppression creates in our lives, and those who want to reshape the distribution of political power and economic resources. To reclaim the personal is to reunite these: to pursue intimacy in a context of liberation; to battle corporations for the individual well-being of everyone. The personal keeps passion alive. A sustained personal life means attention to what kinds of relationships we need in order to remember our goodness, what kind of community keeps us strong, what nourishment we require in order to set about undoing the damages inflicted on us by our own encounters with oppression. What we need in order to maintain our integrity.

When Che Guevara said that the true revolutionary was motivated by love, he prefaced it by saying "At the risk of seeming ridiculous," because love, as a force that is spiritual, personal and creative, is subject to ridicule. Love is subversive, undermining the propaganda of narrow self-interest. Love emphasizes connection, responsibility and the joy we take in each other. Therefore love (as opposed to unthinking devotion) is a danger to the status quo and we have been taught to find it embarrassing.

Art, like dreaming, is something so necessary to internal balance that people deprived of it go a little wacky. Art is the collective dreamplace, the reservoir of our deepest understandings and desires and hopes, as essential as water. In recognition of this fact, the marketplace offers us entertainment, hoping to replace the wild and forested interior of our souls with potted plastic plants. Just as we dream—whether we want to or not, whether we long for or fear our dreaming—people make art and are drawn to art. It's just something our psyches need, even in the most life-denying environments conceivable—drawings made with burnt matches on cigarette papers in the secret prisons of the Argentine junta, poetry carved with nails into the walls of the Angel Island immigrant detention center in San Francisco Bay, songs passed along in whispers from half-buried cellars in the ruins of the Warsaw ghetto. Every vital social movement immediately begins to generate art—songs, poetry, posters, murals, novels—an outpouring of the creativity that people will create from even the smallest crumbs of hope.

Because art, like sex, is an essential and affirming part of aliveness, it cannot be totally repressed. So, as best they can, our rulers steal it, commodify it and return it in barely recognizable form, sanitized, rootless, artificial, or they try to medicate away the need, substituting addiction. People who are deprived of literal dreaming eventually begin to experience waking nightmares and hallucinations. (Ask any parent of a newborn!) We who believe in freedom, whose daily lives are made up of the clash between what we want for this world and the violent greed that surrounds us, need a culture rich in our people's dreams to keep us sane.

Human beings seek integrity like water seeks its level, grow toward creative and just solutions like plants grow toward sunlight, sometimes by crooked paths, but always reaching. If in the midst of these wars we inhabit, in which everything is at stake (and, as Michael Parenti says, all the ruling class has ever wanted is absolutely everything), we can invent and recapture the means to make a sustainable culture of resistance, a way of life as portable as a canteen and deep as a well, then we'll make it. Not each of us, but all of us. Because as powerful as the wielders of death appear, in the end life is stronger.

Index

About the Author

Poet, essayist and historian Aurora Levins Morales was raised a red-diaper baby in the hills of Puerto Rico by her Jewish and Puerto Rican parents. She is the author of *Getting Home Alive*, is a multi-genre work co-written with her mother, Rosario Morales, and *Remedios*, a prose poetry retelling of the history of the Atlantic world, through the lives of Puerto Rican women. Her essays have appeared in *Ms.*, *Women's Review of Books* and numerous anthologies. She holds a doctorate in Women's Studies and History and lectures nationally.

In *Medicine Stories*, she addresses core issues of imperialism and internalized oppression, with particular insight drawn from her personal experience of torture during childhood. Weaving a pattern from her roots in Puerto Rico and Chicago, her ancestral homes in New York's barrio and the shtetls of the Ukraine, with accents drawn from her current homes in Berkeley and Minneapolis and beyond, Levin Morales' writing engages and inspires women and men who are ready to take responsibility for knowing and changing history.

About South End Press

South End Press is a nonprofit, collectively run book publisher with over 200 titles in print. Since our founding in 1977, we have worked to encourage critical thinking and constructive action on the key social, economic, and ecological issues shaping life in the United States and in the world. In this way, we hope to give expression to a wide diversity of democratic social movements and to provide an alternative to the products of corporate publishing.

Through the Institute for Social and Cultural Change, South End Press works with other political media projects—*Z Magazine*; Speakout, a speakers' bureau; and Alternative Radio—to expand access to information and critical analysis. If you would like a free catalog of South End Press books, please write to us at: South End Press, 7 Brookline Street, #1, Cambridge, MA 02139. Visit our website at http://www.lbbs.org.

Related Titles

Zapata's Disciple: Essays
by Martín Espada

De Colores Means All of Us: Latina Views for a Multi-Colored Century
by Elizabeth Martínez

The Last Generation: Poetry and Prose
by Cherríe Moraga

Colonial Dilemma: Critical Perspectives on Contemporary Puerto Rico
edited by Edwin Meléndez and Edgardo Meléndez

Doña Licha's Island: Modern Colonialism in Puerto Rico
by Alfredo López